Edward Sherman Gould

Good English

Or, popular errors in language. Sixth Edition

Edward Sherman Gould

Good English
Or, popular errors in language. Sixth Edition

ISBN/EAN: 9783337084363

Printed in Europe, USA, Canada, Australia, Japan

Cover: Foto ©ninafisch / pixelio.de

More available books at **www.hansebooks.com**

GOOD ENGLISH;

OR,

POPULAR ERRORS IN LANGUAGE.

BY

EDWARD S. GOULD,

AUTHOR OF "ABRIDGEMENT OF ALISON'S EUROPE," ETC., ETC.

SIXTH EDITION.

"POLONIUS. What do you read, my lord?
"HAMLET. Words, words, words!"

NEW YORK:
W. J. WIDDLETON, PUBLISHER.
1875.

Entered according to Act of Congress, in the year 1867,

BY W. J. WIDDLETON,

in the Clerk's Office of the District Court of the United States for the Southern District of New York.

PREFACE.

MANY of the following hints on philology have already appeared in print, in the form of occasional contributions, through a series of years, to newspapers and periodical publications,— chiefly in the *New York Evening Post*. They are now, for the first time, brought together in a volume.

Several books on philology, a part of them of English authorship, have, in the interim, been published in the United States; and some of them have occupied portions of the same ground as is here reviewed. But the author of this book has borrowed nothing for its pages from any source other than his own previous essays, except in those instances where he mentions the fact of borrowing, or quoting.

He makes that remark, however, to disclaim direct borrowing from other books of philological criticism; not to claim originality, properly so called, for anything in his own book: for, in the nature of the case, philological criticism is nothing more than a re-assertion of principles, which are much older than is any one who now writes or reads them. If there is anything strictly "original" in such criticisms, it is limited to a mere selection of subjects, — the subjects themselves being the handiwork of the people.

On that point, it is proper to say that the author has not extended his comments beyond such errors in language as are familiar to everybody, — such errors as are strictly popular, — and which, unfortunately, are to be found in the pages of nearly all of those who are termed good writers. Possible, or imaginary, errors do not seem to be worth the trouble of exposure or refutation.

In the winter of 1865, at the request of his friend, the Right Reverend WILLIAM BACON STEVENS, Bishop of Pennsylvania, the author delivered three lectures on Clerical Elocution, before the Divinity School of the Protestant Episcopal Church, in Philadelphia. The lectures consisted of written precepts, and illustrative readings from the Bible and Prayer Book. The former part was afterward published in the Boston *Church Monthly*, and was thence transferred to the New York *Christian Times*. But copies of the lectures, beyond what the regularly printed numbers of those periodicals could supply, have often been called for; and the author has therefore added them to his philological comments. They are reproduced in the latter part of this volume.

There is this further reason for such reproduction: Elocution is, practically, quite as little understood as is philology; and, as both subjects are proper to be learned by the same persons, they may appropriately both be discussed in the same volume,— which is one of its publisher's educational series.

NEW YORK, February 5th, 1867.

ADVERTISEMENT TO THE FIFTH EDITION.

My publisher says to me that, although several books on philology have been issued since this volume appeared in 1867, this, nevertheless, "holds its own," and continues to be called for; and, as he is about to put another edition to press, he inquires whether I have any additions or alterations to propose.

As to additions: many things of more or less importance were omitted in the original compilation; but additions to a stereotyped book involve reconstruction; and that is more of an undertaking than seems at present advisable.

As to alterations: several slight changes were made after the first edition was published, at the suggestion of my critics; and they were specified in the course of my controversy with Mr. Moon, in the columns of *The Round Table*. I have seen no reason for any further changes.

Some typographical errors or verbal inadvertencies have been discovered in each of the preceding editions of the book, all of which have at last yielded to careful proof-reading; and, in that respect, I believe that the volume now needs no corrections.

E. S. G.

New York, July, 1871.

CONTENTS.

	PAGE
INTRODUCTORY	1
WHO IS RESPONSIBLE	7
SPURIOUS WORDS	11
MISUSED WORDS	28
A PLEA FOR THE QUEEN'S ENGLISH	115
WEBSTER'S ORTHOGRAPHY	137
CLERICAL ELOCUTION	171
INDEX	225

GOOD ENGLISH.

INTRODUCTORY.

The present age is pre-eminently an age of progress; and, unfortunately, the progress is not limited to "things of good report." Error follows fast upon the footsteps of truth, and sometimes truth is left behind in the race.

For example, the English language, within the last quarter of a century, through the agency of good writers, critics and lexicographers, has in many respects been greatly improved; but, through the heedlessness of those who should be its conservators, and the recklessness of those who have been, and are, its corrupters, it has deteriorated in other respects in a greater proportion.

The responsibility for this condition of things rests, mainly, on those who are called "our good writers"; but, to some extent, it rests on all writers, good and bad. How this happens, is easily shown.

Take, for instance, the innovations on our vocabulary. These are of two kinds: the fabrication of new words, and the new use of old words.

And each of those kinds has two causes or sources, — education and ignorance.

An educated man originates a word. He improvises it from a foreign source, or by sound induction from a vernacular root; and, if the word satisfies a want, it is adopted by good writers, and is thenceforward recognized as a valuable addition to the language.

Again, the educated man, by referring to the antecedents of a familiar word, may discover a meaning more or less different from its previously accepted signification; and, by using it in its new sense, he, again, enriches the language.

But it is to be observed that, in each of those cases, the burden of proof in support of his innovation, is *on him*. He must show that the word is properly formed, and is *needed*.

On the other hand, an ignorant man who catches a word by its sound, without knowing its spelling or its signification, — and who, therefore, usually mistakes both, — will reproduce the word in a wrong shape or with a wrong meaning.

Then, as the tendency of things corrupt is to *rise* in a flowing stream, a partially educated man encounters this philological novelty in the popular current, and adopts it *as* a novelty and a convenience; but without actually *knowing* anything more about it than his predecessor did: as your poor judge of currency takes whatever is offered — the genuine and the spurious alike — and pockets and passes them indiscriminately.

Next, one after another, of better educated men, gives the novelty his sanction, — carelessly receives and circulates the "counterfeit presentment," — until finally the best writers, with kindred want of reflection, accept it from the last holder, and mix it up, and pay it out, with their own standard currency. And *thus* errors increase and multiply.

Here, again, the fabricator is responsible for his innovation, and the burden of proof is on him. But, when the case comes to be investigated, it is found that, although the fabricator is responsible in the sense of being *liable* to respond, he is by no means responsible in the sense of being *able* to respond. That is to say, he cannot justify his innovation. His *word* was spurious originally, and he cannot remove its taint, nor can any subsequent indorsement purify it.

These remarks are true, in particular, of spuriously fabricated words; but, also, they are true generally as to every other corruption of language. The errors almost universally originate with ignorant men; and they become current only by reason of their careless adoption by men of education.

As a general rule, the usage of good writers is held to be the common law of a language. Such usage, therefore, is *prima facie* evidence of the accuracy of a disputed word or phrase. But the final proof of accuracy cannot be established by usage; because the writer, in any particular instance, may have been guilty of carelessness; he may have used the word or phrase inadvertently; and if it is fairly presumable that, were his attention called to the point, he would admit the error, his example cannot be permitted to justify what sound philological principles must condemn. In other words, the records of usage are liable to review, and therefore usage is not the court of last resort.

There are, however, many persons who dispute that proposition: persons who lack sensibility to the evils of corruption in philology; who think the purposes of language are fulfilled, when a speaker or writer has made himself understood; who regard conservative views in philology as obstinate adherence to the past; and whose principles, if they can be called such, would go to the extreme of justifying error itself by erroneous precedents. Such reasoning can lead to nothing but literary anarchy.

Yet the most reckless of such cavillers must make a stand somewhere. For example, he cannot shut his eyes to the very rudiments of grammar. He dares not deny that syntax is subject to grammatical rules. He must admit the necessity of concord between verbs and nouns in the matters of number and person, as well as the submission of cases to the government of verbs and prepositions. And so forth. And, if he does admit such necessity, he must further admit that no amount of usage can supersede it.

But nothing is easier than to show, by multitudinous quotations, that the pages of our best writers are thickly sprinkled with violations of the plainest grammatical rules. A careful collector of such curiosities of literature might readily fill a large volume with them. For the purpose of present illustration, some occasional specimens must suffice.

GIBBON says,

" The *use* of fraud and perfidy, of cruelty and injustice, *were* often subservient to the propagation of the faith."

" The *richness* of her arms and apparel *were* conspicuous in the foremost ranks."

JUNIUS says,

" *Both* minister and magistrate *is* compelled to choose between *his* duty and *his* reputation."

" *Neither* Charles nor his brother *were* qualified to support such a system."

BLAIR says,

" The boldness, freedom, and variety of our blank verse *is* infinitely more favorable than rhyme to all kinds of sublime poetry."

MACAULAY says,

" The poetry and eloquence of the Augustan age *was* assiduously studied in Mercian and Northumbrian monasteries."

ADDISON says,

" I do not mean that I think *any one* to blame for taking due care of *their* health."

DRYDEN says,

" Hence, the reason is perspicuous why no French plays when translated *have*, or ever can, *succeed* on the English stage."

Latham says,

"The following facts *may* or have been *adduced* as reasons on the other side."

Johnson says,

"How happy is it that *neither* of us *were* ill in the Hebrides."

And so on, through the whole catalogue of the best English writers, each furnishing scores of instances.

In the cases here cited, the mere quotation of the passages suffices; because everybody knows the grammatical rules that govern in the premises, and therefore no person would undertake to defend the errors on the ground of usage. Besides, no person can doubt that, had the attention of those authors been called to those errors, they would have admitted them to be errors, as a matter of course.

Upon the same ground, it is here claimed that the various philological errors of the present day are not to be justified by the fact of usage, let the literary status of their authors be what it may.

WHO IS RESPONSIBLE?

SPOKEN language is, in the nature of things, more liable to corruption than written language, for two reasons: there are millions who can speak, but cannot write or read, and their ignorance is their excuse; and, all classes of educated people permit themselves to make blunders in common conversation, which they would never think of putting on paper.

The former class can, in no sense, be held responsible for their philological errors. The latter class are responsible — that is, are *liable* to respond — in proportion to their opportunities for avoiding such errors. And their liability falls on them in the same order as it falls on parties who are held liable on a promissory note, — the last indorser is held first. And that order is obviously just, because the last indorser, by his opportunity of knowing *who* had, before him, indorsed the error, and how it was put in circulation, had the best means of avoiding his liability.

Among writers, those who do the most mischief are the original fabricators of error, to wit: the men generally who write for the newspapers. Next to them, in order, are the authors of the vapid, trashy "sensation novels" of the day.

The individuals belonging to the former of those two classes follow the example of "the Athenians, who spend their time in nothing else but either to tell, or to hear, some new *word*." Or, they may more properly be compared to "the enemy who, while men slept, came and sowed tares among the wheat." Dean Alford, however, has nearly exhausted the newspaper branch of this subject; and, as the topic may not be omitted in a book on philological errors; and as, moreover, no man can safely attempt to improve, or to offer a substitute for the Dean's strictures, the alternative seems to be to copy what the Dean says in "A Plea for the Queen's English," page 244, *et seq.*

"This is mainly owing to the vitiated and pretentious style which passes current in our newspapers. The writers in our journals seem to think that a fact must never be related in print in the same terms in which it would be told by word of mouth. The greatest offenders in this point are the country journals, and, as might be expected, just in proportion to their want of real ability. Next to them comes the London penny press; indeed, it is hardly a whit better; and, highest in the scale, but still by no means free from this fault, the London regular press, — its articles being for the most part written by men of education and talent in the various political circles. The main offence of the newspapers, the head and front of their offending, is, the insisting on calling common things by uncommon names; changing our ordinary short Saxon nouns and verbs for long words derived from the Latin. And when it is remembered that this is very generally done by men for the most part ignorant of the derivation and strict meaning of the words they use, we may imagine what delightful confusion is thus introduced into our language. A Latin word which really has a meaning of its own, and might be a very useful one if confined to that meaning, does duty for some word whose significance extends far wider than its own meaning; and thereby, to common English hearers, loses its own proper force, besides utterly confusing their notions about the thing which its new use intended to represent.

"Our journals seem indeed determined to banish our common Saxon words altogether. You never read in them of a *man*, or a *woman*, or a *child*. A man is an *individual*, or a *person*, or a *party;* a woman is a *female*, or, if unmarried, a *young person*, which expression, in the newspapers, is always of the feminine gender; a child is a *juvenile*, and children *en masse* are expressed by that most odious term, the *rising generation*. . . . .

"The newspaper writers never allow us to *go* anywhere, we always *proceed*. A man going home is set down as *an individual proceeding to his residence*.

"We never *eat*, but always *partake*, even though we happen to eat up the whole of the thing mentioned. . . . . We never hear of a *place;* it is always a *locality*. Nothing is ever *placed*, but *located.* No one lives in *rooms*, but always in *apartments*. No man ever *shows* any feeling, but always *evinces* it."

The Dean quotes several other words, and comments appropriately on their substitution; as,

Commence	*for*	Begin,
Avocation	"	Vocation,
Persuasion	"	Sect,
Sustain a loss	"	Lose,
Experience a sensation	"	Feel,
Accord	"	Award,
Allude to	"	Mention,

and so on. In short, the Dean's comments and specifications show that the fraternity of the press in England are *full-blooded relations* of their American cousins.

Whether reiterated exposures of popular philological errors will lead in any degree toward their correction, remains to be seen. One thing is certain, — that, unless the exposures *are* reiterated, and in some way "kept before the people," the corrupters of the language will carry everything before them.

SPURIOUS WORDS.

Reference was made, in the introductory chapter, to words fabricated by ignorant people, and afterward adopted by people of education. There are not many of them, speaking comparatively; but their number is every day increasing, and if their increase cannot be checked, they will soon be "like the stars, for multitude." In the strict sense of the term, such things are not *words* — certainly not English words — at all. They do not belong to the language. They have been foisted into it by ignorant or assuming persons under false pretences, and they should be summarily ejected.

As a specimen of this class, take first the verb to

JEOPARDIZE.

To *jeopard* is a legitimate English verb, as old as the language. Its etymology is, probably, Fr. *jeu-parti*. It means to put in danger, to expose to loss or injury, to imperil, to hazard, etc.

But some aspiring wight, being ambitious of long words, or apprehensive of the incompleteness of short words, happened to hear it imperfectly; and, fancying that euphony required for it an additional syllable, he improved it into *jeopardize*, and set it afloat with the grave complacency of a man who thinks he has done a good thing. He might just as well have made the same improvement on *hazard* *Hazardize* is as legitimate English as "jeopardize"; and, for that matter, so is *perilize*, or *endangerize*, or any other *ize* that anybody may choose to fabricate from any other verb.

CONTROVERSIALIST.

This is another instance of the counterfeit currency. It probably was first issued in conversation; thence it may have made its way into the newspapers; thence into fashionable novels; and thence — and here, unfortunately, conjecture ends — into the pages of MACAULAY, whose claim to the rank of a "good writer" is altogether beyond question.

If, however, such a man as MACAULAY is to be impeached, and if a word so well accredited as *controversialist* is to be repudiated, the proceedings must be made and had in due form.

By reverting to first principles, we find that an *act* precedes a *fact*. A verb precedes a noun. A man *exists*, and thence *existence;* he *speaks*, and thence *speaker*. In short, whenever a verb and a noun are cognates, the verb is the primitive and the noun is formed from it with some reference to analogous construction. We have, then, in the first place, the verb *controvert*.

Controvert is derived from the Latin *contra*, against, and *vertere*, to turn. And it may be well to remark here, parenthetically, on one of the ten thousand inconsistencies of Noah Webster.

He undertook to *reform* English orthography; and one of his rules was, very properly, that orthography should be controlled by etymology: but, practically, he added the unlucky mental reservation — *whenever he thought such control expedient*. His critics have shown that he violated the rule almost as often as he followed it, in troublesome cases. The inconsistency is this.

Webster gives nearly twenty primitive words, besides all their derivatives, commencing with the Latin *contra*, as *contradict, contravene*, etc., and he spells them all with the *a, contra*. But although the root of "controvert" is the same *contra*, he leaves it in a state of non-conformity both to analogy and to his rule. If Webster had "reformed" this word, "controvert"; that is, if he had *restored* it to what one would think must have been its original orthography, — contravert, — he would, for once, have made rather a happy hit, and, probably, escaped censure.

But, to return from this digression. We have

    Controvert, the verb.
    Controverter, ⎫
    Controvertist, ⎬ nouns.
    Controversy, ⎭
    Controversial, ⎫ adjectives.
    Controvertible, ⎭
    Controversially, ⎫ adverbs.
    Controvertibly, ⎭

But where or whence *controversialist?*

It is formed by adding *ist* to the adjective; and the question arises, whether a noun can properly be formed from an adjective by the addition of *ist*, when such formation is made in disregard of the primitive verb?

A noun may be so formed from an adjective, when it has no primitive verb; as, for example, *sensual, sensualist*. And perhaps that distinction may be the rule in the premises. At any rate, although Paley did once use the word, Johnson ignores it, and even Webster,* as recently as 1856, repudiates it.

The philosophy of the thing would seem to be, that definitions must, to some extent, control derivatives, and the formation of a noun must conform to the attribute or prerogative of its antecedent verb.

---

* " Webster " here, and in some other instances, is used conventionally. " Webster's Dictionary," since its publication in 1828, has passed through a series of revolutions and " reconstructions," especially in the matter of orthography, and those processes were continued after the lexicographer's death, in 1843; two or more altered editions having been published since that event. The *last* edition differs from all of its predecessors much more than they differ from each other. For instance, the etymologies and definitions are, in the last edition, almost entirely remodelled or renewed: a proceeding that has greatly increased the value of the work; but which would seem, in the same proportion, to have repudiated the precedent labours of Webster himself and to have detracted from his reputation as a lexicographer. Webster's detestable spelling of a hundred words — more or less — is retained; but even that is in many cases presented alternatively with correct orthography; so that, on the whole, the present title of the Dictionary is a matter of courtesy rather than a matter of fact.

For example, a *separatist* is one who separates; an *economist*, one who economizes: but a *controversialist* is not, and cannot be, one who *controversials*, because there is no such act and no such verb. Hence, the word seems to be a malformation; and, being a word that no scholar would deliberately fabricate, it must have originated in ignorance and have been accredited through inadvertence. And as, besides, the word is not *needed* (for we already have the true word, *controvertist*, which is properly formed and expresses the meaning), and is not in such common use as to create a necessity for a synonyme to avoid repetition, — no good writer can be justified in using it.

LENIENCY.

This is a word — if, as previously suggested, it deserves to be called a " word " — which is not needed in our language; — which is not justified by the precedents of our language; — which did not originate with educated men; — and which should not receive the sanction of educated men.

The thing meant to be expressed by the word is *lenity*, and lenity is English. It is derived from *lenitas*. Beginning with Johnson, we have

              Lenity, noun.
              Lenient, adjective.

Also,
      Lenient, ⎫
      Lenitive, ⎬ nouns. ⎫ medical
      Lenitive, adjective. ⎭   ⎭ terms.

But, when we come to Webster, we find,

Lenience, } noun,
Leniency, }

though, indeed, with very brief notice. He gives no authority. He says, merely, by way of definition, lenity, clemency.

Worcester, unfortunately, goes further and fares worse. He says,

Lenience, } The quality of being len-
Leniency, }   ient, etc. *Ed. Rev.*

That is, no etymology given, but the *Edinburgh Review* cited. The *Edinburgh Review* is undoubtedly high authority; and, as Worcester cites it, he must have found the word — that is, *one* of the words — somewhere in it. What Worcester *meant* by giving two such philological abortions, when surely one was too much, the reader must conjecture. And it is worthy of a passing remark, that, while Webster was content with giving but one — *leniency* — in the edition of 1856, he, in order not to be behind his American rival, copied or borrowed *lenience* from Worcester, in the "*last* Revised," 1866. " without," as the newspapers say, " giving credit."

But the *ipse dixit* — or, perhaps, more properly, the *lapsus pennæ* — of one man, even if that man is a writer in the Edinburgh Review, cannot make *leniency* a good English word. It lacks what is here claimed as essential to legitimacy. It is not properly constructed and it is not needed. Its place is already occupied by the legal proprietor, and its last syllable is akin in vulgarism to the *ize* of "jeopardize," and the *ist* of "controversialist."

There is a necessity for insisting strenuously on this point, because the present tendency of philological corruption is strong in the direction of multiplying words by accumulating final syllables.

A book called "John Halifax" is what merchants would call "a fair average specimen" of contemporaneous and "unreadable" novels. Its author cannot claim rank as a good writer, in the sense of a philological authority; but he (or *she*, perhaps) writes as well as the majority of authors in that particular branch of writing — and he has readers enough to make his example pernicious, if it is bad.

In that book, one may find, among other vulgarisms, *conversationalist* and *experimentalize*. And if one will take the trouble to look into Webster's *last* Dictionary, he will find that the compilers of that work — true to the modern system of making each new dictionary contain "ten thousand (more or less) words not contained in any rival work" — have duly recorded the Halifax-additions to their vocabulary. They had the grace to note the latter word as "*rare*," — which, let us all hope, it may continue to be!

And yet, the compilers aforesaid, but half — indeed, much less than half — "improved their opportunity." For if "conversationalist" and "experimentalize" are legitimate words, there is no

Websterian reason for refusing them such *legitimate* descendants as

>Conversationalistic,*
>Conversationalistically,
>Conversationalisticability,
>Conversationalisticableness;

>Experimentalizer,
>Experimentalizistical,
>Experimentalizistically,
>Experimentalizisticability,
>Experimentalizisticableness.

In *short* — if that word can be permitted to appear on the same page with those philological Titans — there would seem to be no assignable limit to the tagging on of unmeaning syllables, except the width of a page.

There certainly is *no* limit to the manufacture of new words by the addition of syllables to old

---

* The Hon. George P. Marsh, unquestionably an accomplished philologist, wrote for *The Nation* — a weekly literary paper of a high order of literary merit — a series of articles on Webster's Dictionary; and in such articles one would naturally look for great accuracy, not only of criticism, but of style.

Occasion will be taken, on a subsequent page, to refer again to Mr. Marsh. He is mentioned here for the purpose of showing his use of a word similar to those above specified. His sentence is (*The Nation*, Sept. 20, 1866):—

"In this instance — the first, I suppose, in which the word 'sensuous' occurs — it probably meant, suggestive of images of things perceptible by the senses; picturesque, *materialistic*."

Would not *material* have answered the purpose of a scholar like Mr. Marsh, especially when he was criticising a dictionary?

words, if we once admit the principle of *equality* in the republic of letters. If, in that republic, one man's *word* is as good as another's, those who assent to *leniency*, cannot refuse, by and by, to recognize such vulgarisms as

>Preventative,
>Rotatory,
>Casuality,

and so forth. Those "words," and many others akin to them, are already in constant oral use among ignorant people, and they are gradually working their way up among people of some education. And, in the nature of the case, there is no assignable reason why they should not eventually get into our newspapers, books, and dictionaries. Indeed, *rotatory* has already done so.

UNDERHANDED.

This "word" is formed by adding to the adjective *underhand* a participial termination; but the addition still leaves the word an adjective, without in the least modifying the sense of the true word. There is no verb *to* underhand, and no noun *an* underhand, from which such a compound could be made. The addition of *ed*, therefore, renders the word a mere vulgarism; as much so as the same addition would make of *beforehand* and *behindhand*.

What would be said of *behindhanded?* Or, take a shorter word, *bland* — and make it *blanded*.

Yet, strange to say, Worcester accredits the word and cites Smart, and Webster cites Coleridge! — two strong names on a philological question. But the indorsement is not strong enough to make the word good. It is no better than *leniency*, *jeopardize*, etc.

In the same style of corruption, but, perhaps, a little lower in the scale, is the addition of a syllable to *undermine*. This corruption has not yet made its appearance in newspapers and dictionaries, but it is very common in the conversation of a certain class of people, and may be considered " a candidate for admission" into the dictionaries, by and by. The people who misuse the word seem to think that its primary formation is *undermind*, and they therefore have no difficulty in saying, " he *underminded* them."

DONATE.

Here is another intruder into the family circle, which " has not on a wedding garment."

Webster, of course, records the word; and he gravely gives its etymology, " from *donare*, *donatum*," etc., — as if the prig who fabricated that bit of literature ever saw a Latin dictionary, or ever heard of the Latin language!

There is something intensely farcical in that solemn etymology. It must have been intended for a sly joke. All the world knows that Johnson introduced a sly joke into *his* dictionary, when he defined the word " lexicographer "; and it seems that Webster, in imitation of his illustrious predecessor, has introduced *his* sly joke in the etymology of *donate*.

Mr. Richard Grant White, who is well known as an accurate philologist, not long ago published in the *New York Evening Post* an indignant protest against " donate " ; to which somebody, with perhaps equal indignation, but by no means with equal ability, responded, by elaborately defending *donation*, and adding, that " no objection could be urged against the proscribed word which would not apply with equal force against *donation*." The writer of these pages thereupon " volunteered his services " to the following effect : —

Certain " eatables," spread on a table on certain occasions, constitute what is termed a *collation*. Would you say to a friend who, with you, was standing near that table, " Come, let us *collate?* " Or, if an *ovation* were about to be offered to a great military captain, would you say, " We intend to *ovate* General Grant to-morrow ? " Or, again, if Mr. Everett were about to deliver his *oration* on Washington, at the Academy of Music, would you say, " Let us go to hear Everett *orate?* "

" Donate,' then, may be dismissed with this remark : so long as its place is occupied by *give, bestow, grant, present*, etc., it is not needed ; and it should be unceremoniously bowed out, or thrust out, of the seat into which it has, temporarily, intruded.

AUTHORESS, ETC.

There is yet another instance of this propensity to fabricate new words by the addition of a syllable ; but it is not altogether so modern as some of the preceding cases. That is, the addition of *ess* to those nouns which indicate persons, in order to designate females.

The entire number of English words denoting persons, which properly take the *ess* for such designation, is very small. And a majority of those are *titles*, where the discrimination is a matter of necessity; as *abbess, baroness, duchess, countess, empress, princess, marchioness*, etc. Or, they are words of which the primary words are suggestive of men, and which therefore require the change when they are applied to women; as, *ambassador, governor, hunter, priest, prophet*, etc.

In addition to these, there are some words which long usage has sanctioned, although a good reason can hardly be given for their admission into our vocabulary, because the primary words serve all the purposes of their substitutes. Of these, are *actor, actress; benefactor, benefactress; patron, patroness*.

But there is a class of words, some of them modern, and most of them of very recent fabrication, which sets all philological principles at defiance. Two of them that are the least objectionable to ourselves, because they are the most familiar to our ears, are *poetess* and *authoress;* but, philologically, they are just as absurd as any of their successors.

Poet means, simply, a person who writes poetry; and *author*, in the sense under consideration, a person who writes poetry or prose: not a *man* who writes, but a *person* who writes. Nothing, in either word, indicates sex; and everybody knows that the functions of both poets and authors are common to both sexes. Hence, "authoress" and "poetess" are superfluous. And they are superfluous, also, in another respect, — that they are very rarely used, indeed they hardly *can* be used, independently of the *name* of the writer; as, Mrs., or Miss, or a female Christian name. They are, besides, philological absurdities, because they are fabricated on the false assumption that their primaries indicate *men*. They are, moreover, liable to the charge of affectation and prettiness, to say nothing of pedantic pretension to accuracy.

If, however, those two words have, by long usage, become conventionally endurable; what shall be said of the superfine affectation, prettiness, and pedantry of *conductress, directress, inspectress, waitress*, and so on, which have become as plenty as blackberries?

Conductor is a *person* who conducts; director, a person who directs; inspector, a person who inspects; waiter, a person who waits. Yet if the *ess* is to be a permitted or an endured addition to those words, there is no reason in language or in logic for excluding it from *any* noun that indicates a person; and the next editions of our dictionaries may be made complete by the addition of *writeress, officeress, manageress, superintendentess, secretaryess, treasureress, singeress, walkeress, talkeress*, and so on, to the end of the vocabulary.

FIRSTLY.

This is still another word of the class with the tagged syllable. It is frequently used by those who may be called good writers. Even Dickens, whose style is far above that of novel-writers generally, often uses it. There is no need of expending time or argument on "firstly." No lexicographer has yet ventured to accredit it; and Webster, while inserting it, repudiates it thus, — "improperly, used for *first*."

As an instance of the force of example, and of the facility with which good writers fall into errors of which examples are everywhere current, — a late number of *Blackwood's Magazine* contains "firstly"; and not only that, but in the same paragraph *demean* is used in the sense of *debase:* a subject that will be considered in another chapter.

TOWARD, ETC.

There are several words ending in *ward* which the spirit of innovation has "improved" by the addition — not, indeed, of a syllable, but — of a letter; to wit, the letter *s*. As, toward, towards, etc.

Richardson says, "*Toward* is made up of two Saxon words, *to* and *ward*. *Ward*, or *weard*, is the imperative of the verb *wardian* or *weardian*, to look at, or to direct the view. *Ward* may with propriety be joined to the name of any person, place, or thing, to or from which our sight may be directed," etc.

Hence, we have *backward, forward, toward, upward, onward, downward, hitherward, thitherward, afterward, heavenward, earthward,* and so on. And early English writers have given the words in a separate form; as, for example, the translators of the Bible say *to us ward,* etc.

But where is there a warrant for the addition of the final *s* to any of the words, — excepting its incidental, or perhaps accidental, use by certain old English writers, as Milton, Shakespeare, Dr. South, and others? Those authors are doubtless followed by modern writers without number; but also, one might suppose, without reflection on the part of the writers; and certainly without *our* knowing that the fault may not have been with the *printer.*

The etymology of the word furnishes no pretext for the *s;* its addition is merely arbitrary, — though, also, capricious; for few writers use it uniformly. If any person should seek to defend it, he must carry his defence beyond the immediate cases, and include *anywhere, everywhere, nowhere, anyway, everyway, noway,* and so on. Ignorant usage has already made that addition. In the common parlance of uneducated people, nothing is more common than somewheres, anywheres, anyways, nowheres, etc.; and, as yet, nothing is more vulgar.

STAND-POINT.

But of all the instances in which solemn philological blundering has recently developed itself, *stand-point* stands forth as the bright particular star. It is the very counterpart of Dogberry's "*non com.*" It faintly suggests, by its sound, what the French call "a suspicion" of a meaning; but the moment you investigate the thing and attempt to reach the meaning, you find it a mere will-o'-the-wisp.

The compound is used for *point of view;* but *why*, is not obvious. For if one *means* point of view, why does not one *say* point of view?

"Stand-point" does not mean point of view for two good reasons, one of which suffices; namely, it does not mean anything. It is not an English word. "Stand," by itself, is English; and "point," by itself, is English: but the two words, like certain chemical ingredients, will not unite until a combining medium is introduced between them.

Thus, also, "start," by itself, is English; and so, also, is "point": but is *start-point* anything? Independently of the question of meaning, such combinations are philologically defective. The verbs *stand* and *start*, in those cases, must be changed to adjectives or participles before they can combine with the noun "point."

Stand*ing*-point and start*ing*-point are something. They have a meaning. They are kindred in construction to *landing-place*, and other familiar terms; and they mean, simply, the place, or point, where one stands or whence one starts. "Stand-point," therefore, to be English, should be changed to *standing-point*.

But when the investigator reaches *this* "point,"

he begins to see *the* point; to wit, that *stand*-point certainly does not mean point of *view*, although that is the sense in which it is constantly used. If, however, those persons who have become accustomed to "stand-point" are still too much enamoured with its conciseness to abandon it altogether, an alternative is at hand.

Their chief and sole object being (as it needs must be) to condense "point of view" into one word, of two syllables, irrespectively of accurate philological construction; and since, with them, meaning is nothing and brevity everything, — let them say and write *view-point*. That meets the case and covers the ground. "View-point" is precisely the same sort of English as "stand-point"; and it possesses the substantial advantage of meaning — admitting, for the sake of argument, that it means anything — what the speaker or writer intends to convey by "stand-point."

There is little occasion to comment particularly on the other class of newly-made words; those, namely, that are properly constructed and are needed; because that is a branch of philology that will always assert itself and protect itself. Words of that class bear their own credentials. They need no advocacy and they are safe from criticism.

MISUSED WORDS.

The spurious words are less numerous than the misused words; but in both categories the philological heresy has the same origin, character, and tendency.

BESIDE. BESIDES.

Our lexicographers have contented themselves with leaving these two words as they find them in the pages of good and bad writers — jumbled together without any attempt at discrimination between them. But, as such discrimination is important, the writer of this volume, having failed to find a satisfactory elucidation of the subject in any work on philology then within his reach, ventured to suggest the following solution of the difficulty through the medium of the *New York Evening Post*, in or about the year 1856.

Beside is a preposition, meaning, originally, *by the side of;* as,

"The lovely Thais sits *beside* thee";

and usage has modified, or extended, that meaning to *one side*, or, *out of the regular course;* as,

"It is *beside* my present business to pursue the minor points of the argument."

And it has been further modified to *out of*, or, *in a state of deviation from;* as,

"Paul, thou art *beside* thyself."

Again, *besides* is also a preposition when it means in *addition to ;* as,

"*Besides* all this, between us and you there is a great gulf fixed."

And, finally, *besides* is an adverb, when it means *moreover ;* as,

"Set you down this ;
And say, *besides*, that in Aleppo once,
When a malignant and a turbaned Turk," etc.

The sum of the matter, then, is,— that *beside* is *always* a preposition, and only a preposition. *Besides*, also, is a preposition when it means *in addition to ;* but when it means *moreover*, it is an adverb.

Hence, not only is the use of *beside* as an adverb an error, but the error is aggravated by its taint of affectation: it smacks of attempted prettiness in style. And that painful result also ensues when the preposition meaning *in addition to* is deprived of its *s*. These are the two examples:—

"And *beside* all this, between us and you there is a great gulf."

"And say, *beside*, that in Aleppo once."

In a preceding paragraph, it is remarked that our lexicographers have left these two words as they found them, etc. That was true at the time it was written. But the last edition of Webster (1866) has the following comments, which, in substance, are nearly identical with what was thus written in 1856. They are reproduced here for the twofold purpose of relieving the writer of this book from a suspicion of plagiarism; and to show that his views, as then expressed, are so far corroborated: —

"*Beside. Besides.* These words, whether used as prepositions or adverbs, have been considered strictly synonymous from an early period of our literature and have been freely interchanged by our best writers. There is, however, a tendency in present usage to make the following distinction between them. 1. That *beside* be used only and always as a preposition, with the original meaning *by the side of;* as, to sit *beside* a fountain; or, with the closely allied meaning *aside from*, or *out of;* as, this is *beside* our present purpose: 'Paul, thou art *beside* thyself.' The adverbial sense to be wholly transferred to the cognate word. 2. That *besides*, as a preposition, take the remaining sense, *in addition to;* as, *besides* all this; *besides* the considerations here offered: 'There was a famine in the land *besides* the first famine.' And that it also take the adverbial sense of *moreover, beyond*, etc., which had been divided between the words; as, *besides*, there are other considerations which belong to this case."

LADY. WIFE.

The word *lady*, as a substitute for *wife*, is a snobbish vulgarism, which may have originated with a clerk in a hotel.

Mr. and Mrs. Somebody arrived at the hotel, and the clerk officiously recorded their names — "Mr. Somebody and *Lady*."

Nevertheless, the word *wife*, as Cæsar says of the polar star,

> "Has no fellow in the firmament."

It has neither synonyme nor substitute; and any attempt to fabricate either, is a sort of philological affront to the original.

On the other hand, *lady* is, to a certain extent, interchangeable with *woman*. As a descriptive term, it serves to discriminate between the orders of society; and, so far forth, it indicates position, cultivation, refinement. Yet it is by no means essentially the superior word. For example,

> "O *woman*, in our hours of ease,
> Uncertain, coy, and hard to please,
> When pain and anguish wring the brow,
> A ministering angel thou."

And, in Portia's reply to Brutus, Julius Cæsar, Act II. Sc. 1:—

> "*Brutus.* You are my true and honourable wife;
>   As dear to me as are the ruddy drops
>   That visit this sad heart.
> *Portia.* If this were true, then should I know this secret.
>   I grant, I am a *woman*; but, withal,
>   A *woman* that Lord Brutus took to wife.
>   I grant I am a *woman*; but, withal,
>   A *woman* well reputed,—Cato's daughter.
>   Think you, I am no stronger than my sex,
>   Being so fathered and so husbanded?"

In cases like those, *lady* would make but a sorry figure as a substitute for *woman*.

But, in the case of the other Portia — Merchant of Venice, Act III. Sc. 3 — *woman* would fare quite as indifferently : —

> "*Bassanio.*   Gentle *lady*,
> When I did first impart my love to you,
> I freely told you, all the wealth I had
> Ran in my veins; I was a gentleman;
> And then I told you true. And yet, dear *lady*,
> Rating myself at nothing, you shall see
> How much I was a braggart."

The result is, then, that in a personal address, as in Bassanio's instance, *lady* is the indispensable word; and it is also indispensable as a descriptive or discriminating term. But, as the synonyme of *wife*, it is an unwarrantable and depreciating vulgarism, quite unbecoming educated people.

COUPLE.

Couple, as the synonyme of *two*, is a more difficult subject than *lady*, because it has the support of more general, if not higher, authority.

The noun *couple* is necessarily the result of the verb *to couple.* The act of coupling precedes the fact of being coupled, and therefore the meaning of the noun is controlled by the meaning of the verb.

The verb, etymologically and by the dictionaries, means *to link, chain, fasten,* or *connect* one thing with another, and those definitions provide for all possible cases of *two joined.*

Again, the noun is thus defined in our dictionaries :

"Two things of the same kind connected together; a pair; a brace. A male and female connected by betrothal or marriage."

Hence, *any* "two," on being fastened, chained, joined, linked, connected together, become a *couple;* and any two *not* joined, etc., are *not* a couple.

Certain other words are used, in a sort of technical sense, to signify *two together*, or two *alike*, but not necessarily *united;* as, a *pair*, a *brace*, a *yoke* (of oxen), and, in American English, referring to horses, a *span*.

These words, in their appropriate connections, all designate two things having something in common. Yet, while these words — not one of which necessarily involves the fact of two *united* — are always used discriminately, and never as the mere synonyme of *two; couple*, which does inevitably involve the fact of two united, is used *in*discriminately as the synonyme of two, and in reference to things that are never united!

People of all classes, and writers of all positions, without the slightest misgiving, compunction, or remorse, daily fabricate such phrases as a *couple of days*, a *couple of dollars*, a *couple of eggs*, a *couple of books*, a *couple of weeks, months*, or *years;* and so on, to the end of English nouns-substantive.

And for all that, those very people and those very writers would laugh to scorn any man who ventured to say, a *brace* of days, weeks, months, or years; a *yoke* of eggs; a *pair* of dollars; a *span* of books.

But, notwithstanding the laugh and the scorn, the latter phrases are not only no worse than the former, but they are more nearly correct than the former, because they do not involve an absurdity.

A *pair* of days, for example, is a physical possibility; for the two days may be essentially alike, and as near together — before, after, or by the side of each other — as two things can be: but a *couple* of days is a physical *im*possibility, because the two days cannot be "linked or fastened together." And that is substantially true of the other "couples" here designated; as, eggs, dollars, and books — which, indeed, *might* be linked or fastened together, but which in fact never are so.

DEMEAN.

This word is often used in the sense of *debase* — a blunder which has no better apology for its existence than the fact that the second syllable of the word, when separated from the first, signifies something akin to debasement: just as the second syllable of *deride*, when separated from the first, signifies taking a ride! Or, again — which is more immediately applicable — as *meaning* might be used in the place of *grovelling*.

The verb *demean* and the noun *demeanour* have a common signification: to behave, to conduct, well or ill; behaviour, conduct, good or bad.

If an educated man were to set about attaching a new meaning to the verb, he would see the necessity of attaching a cognate meaning to the noun. If he made *demean* signify *debase*, he must make *demeanour* signify *debasement*, or base conduct; the absurdity of which is, or should be, sufficient to dispose of the question.

The lexicographers have very indifferently discharged their duty in regard to *demean*.

Johnson gives *debase* as a secondary definition, and cites Shakespeare as one who used the word in that sense. But when the reader goes behind Johnson's certificate, he finds that Johnson is at fault.

The antecedents of the quoted line, Comedy of Errors, Act IV. Sc. 3,

"Else he would never so *demean* himself,"

show that Shakespeare's meaning *debase* by "demean," is arbitrarily assumed by Johnson. Any person can see for himself, by examining the passage, that if *behave*, or *conduct*, were substituted for " demean,"

"Else he would never so *behave* himself,"
"Else he would never so *conduct* himself,"

the sense of the line would remain unchanged.

Webster blindly follows Johnson as to the definition and authority, but he introduces a blunder of his own by adding "*not used*." It certainly *is* "used," frequently, and by men of education. The "use" is a matter of common observation among all persons who take notice of language.

Worcester gives the same definition, and cites

Doddridge: and Worcester is at least correct in his citation. But the passage quoted is one of religious rhapsody, in which the writer may not have paused much on the selection of words. Besides, Doddridge may be better authority as a theologian than as a philologist.

At any rate, until the advocates of the "*debase*" definition are prepared to accept its consequence,— that then *demeanour* means *debasement*, or, more properly, *base conduct*,— further argument may be safely postponed.

CONSEQUENCE.

This word is constantly used by everybody in the sense of *importance;* although, etymologically, there is nothing in common between the two words.

Consequence comes from the Latin *consequentia* and the French *conséquence;* which, respectively, come from the Latin prefix *con* and the Latin verb *sequor*, to follow. The chief element of the noun is, therefore, *sequence*, a *result*, something that *follows*.

On the other hand, *importance* refers to things of moment in themselves, independently of what follows.

Yet here, also, the lexicographers are very much in fault.

Johnson gives as a seventh and final definition of "consequence," *importance, moment;* and again he cites Shakespeare erroneously. He quotes, in support of his definition, Macbeth, Act I. Sc. 3 : —

> "But, 't is strange;
> And oftentimes, to win us to our harm,
> The instruments of darkness tell us truths;
> Win us with honest trifles, to betray us
> In deepest *consequence*."

Whereas, in that extract, "consequence" is used in its primary sense, and "deepest" is the word that conveys the sense of "importance." "Deepest consequence" is equivalent to the *direst result;* the most *important sequel*, etc.

The erroneous citation of Johnson thus leaves one in doubt — so far, at least, as the dictionary is concerned — whether the Doctor intended to give his own sanction to the definitions of "demean" and "consequence"; or, merely, to place them in his vocabulary and leave the student to adopt or reject them, according to his own estimate of Shakespeare as an authority. The student has, indeed, the privilege of consulting Johnson's other works, to ascertain whether the lexicographer gives those definitions the sanction of his own practice; but *that* is another matter.

If etymology is to control the point, the result is not doubtful. On that ground, a consequence is a something that follows from an antecedent, or a cause; a following; a result. And in that sense, the familiar phrase "it is of no consequence" — which phrase, with some variations, is the form in which the word is questionably used — is precisely equivalent to "*it is of no following,* or *result*"; which means nothing. It might be made to mean something by a substitution of the verb *has* for the verb *is*, — "it *has no following*," no sequence, no result; but that is not what the speaker, or writer, of the phrase means.

The phrase, however, is now so universally used, and it is so generally accredited by both lexicographers and good writers, that no man can be justified in asserting dogmatically that it is a corruption of language. But it is unquestionably a departure from "first principles," and it may at least be deplored by conservative philologists. Perhaps, now and then, one or more of such persons will avoid the phrase!

PREDICATE.

The verb predicate comes to us from the Latin *prædico-care*, to cry in public, to proclaim; whence, also, comes to *preach*. And to *predict* comes from a similar Latin root, — *præ*, before, and *dico-cere*, to say or tell. All of which goes to show that the functions of the etymological family, whence *predicate* descends, are limited to *speaking*, saying, telling, etc. And our lexicographers generally agree in so limiting the definition of predicate; namely, to say, to affirm, to declare. Webster extends it to "to affirm; to assert to belong to something; as, to *predicate* whiteness of snow." Which is all very well. But Webster, strange to say! adds a secondary definition which shall be quoted in a subsequent paragraph.

Ignorant usage — and *very* ignorant usage it must be — in the United States, has recently paraded predicate in the sense of *to found;* as, "his argument was *predicated* on the assumption," etc.; "my opinion is *predicated* on the belief," and so forth.

The word is used in that sense in the pulpit, at the bar, and *of course* in novels and newspapers. But it no more *means* to found, than it means to *build*, or to *destroy*. And the good people who are aiding in the circulation of this philological imposture might as well say, if they *will* misuse the word,

"Jenkins *predicated* his house in the short space of three months; but it was *predicated* to the ground during the great fire of the 1st of February."

Yet, mad as the people may be on this point, it seems that one lexicographer is "as mad as they." The last Revised Edition of Webster gives as a secondary definition of predicate,

"To rest upon for proof, or as an assertion or an opinion; to found; to base; [U. S.]"

for which profound definition the "U. S." are made responsible.

The events of the last five years have shown to the world that the "U. S." are able to do almost anything; but whether they are "able to respond" to the liability of that definition, is a matter of great doubt in some minds.

Alack! who can hope to stay the progress of corruption in language, when the very men who should be its guardians actually help on the corruption?

EITHER. NEITHER.

Either is an Anglo-Saxon word, having two opposite significations; but with this in common, that each of them refers to *two* objects, and two *only*.

Either means *one or the other* in such phrases as " either Monday or Tuesday"; " either John or Peter," etc. And it means *each* when we say " forests on *either* side of the river."

In the second sense it is, probably, never misused. In the first, it is often applied to more than two; as, " either Monday, Tuesday, or Wednesday"; " either of the twelve jurors," and so on. And this misuse has the sanction of all writers and all lexicographers. The authorities are as nearly unanimous as may be.

Yet, the lexicographers agree in the primary definition of the word. They all say " one or *the* other," which necessarily means of *two*, and *no more*.

And the same remark as to definition is true of *neither;* namely, "*not either*"; "*not* one or *the* other," which word therefore refers, negatively, to *two* and *no more*. Yet it is misused in precisely the same way: " neither Monday, Tuesday, nor Wednesday"; " neither of the twelve jurors," and so forth.

It is marvellous that so palpable an error could have gained so general a circulation; and equally marvellous is it, that men of education will continue to sanction the error.

Look, for a moment, at an illustration. *Either* means one *or* the other; *both* means one *and* the other. Thus, each of them refers to two, and two only. Now, imagine the phrase, "*both* Monday, Tuesday, and Wednesday"; "*both* John, Peter, and James"; "*both* of the twelve jurors." Would any person endure such expressions? Would any amount of *usage* justify them? Yet *both*, in such instances, is quite as correct as *neither* or *either*.

Besides, such a use of "both" is not an imaginary case. Trench, in "English Past and Present," says: "And thus it will come to pass that what seems, and in fact is, the newer swarm, will have many older words, and very often an archaic air and old-world fashion *both* about" [these words should be transposed, — "about both," — which is another blunder of the Dean's] "the words they use, the pronunciation of the words, and the order and manner in which they combine them."

As to *either*, Trench, in the same book, manages to apply it to no less than *five* subjects in this sentence: "*Either* the words were not idiomatic, or were not intelligible, or were not needed, or looked ill, or sounded ill, or some other valid reason existed against them."

In addition to the misuse of *either* and *neither*, these words are both frequently mispronounced; particularly, by clergymen.

The pronunciation of English words is nearly independent of philological rules, and it depends almost altogether on usage. This is proved by a single illustration. If there were any rule in the case, how could the pronunciation of the several words ending in *ough* be otherwise than uniform, instead of their having four entirely distinct sounds — to the horror of all foreigners? Etymology has some influence on orthoëpy *sometimes;* and so, sometimes, has analogy; but, on the whole, custom is supreme.

The lexicographers with great uniformity give the pronunciation of these two words, *ē-ther* and *nē-ther*. Webster says "ē-ther is the pronunciation given in nearly all the English dictionaries, and is still the prevailing one in the United States; *ī-ther* has of late become somewhat common in England. Analogy, however, as well as the best and most general usage, is decidedly in favor of *ē-ther*."

In these circumstances, it is clear that the majority has the best of the argument. For the great preponderance of usage has taken one side of the question; and as there is no philological rule or principle to warrant a change, and as, besides, there is no *need* of a change, the opposing minority become mere schismatics, who can give no higher reason for their action than their own private opinion or caprice; and *that* is a very poor excuse for an innovation.

A common reply, in the United States, to the question, "Why do you say *i-ther* and *ni-ther?*" is, "The words are so pronounced by the best-educated people in England." But that reply is *not true.* That is to say, a majority of the best English usage is not on that side of the question.

All that any man in the United States can *gain* by the pronunciation of *i-ther* and *ni-ther* is the credit, or the discredit, of affectation, or ostentation, — as who should say, "*I* know how they do it in England": for assuredly, that pronunciation is not sanctioned by a majority of *our* best-educated men. The number of those who use it here, is but a very small minority.

In society, *i-ther* and *ni-ther* are not of much moment; because any member of the disapproving majority can "avenge himself" on his learned friend, by rejoining *e-ther* and *ne-ther*. And, at any rate, little inaccuracies and inelegancies — not, however, affectations! — of language may as well be tolerated in common colloquy, because they are inevitable.

But *i-ther* and *ni-ther* in public speaking, and especially in the pulpit, where they are now beginning to take the horrible proportions of *a fashion*, are grievous annoyances to which a helpless audience should not be subjected.

Of all men in the world, a clergyman, in his official capacity, should avoid peculiarity, not to say affectation,* not to say ostentation; and what-

---

* " In man or woman, but far most in man,
    And most of all in man that ministers
    And serves the altar, in my soul I loathe
    All *affectation*. 'T is my perfect scorn;
    Object of my implacable disgust."
                                                COWPER.

ever his "private judgment" may be, as to the merits of the question, the fact remains, that *i-ther* and *ni-ther* smack strongly of those qualities, and therefore they "are not expedient."

PARAPHERNALIA.

The constant misuse of this word has caused it almost entirely to lose its original signification. It is a law-term and only a law-term, originally; and it so continues. Any use of it, out of the law, cannot be appropriate. A *man* cannot have paraphernalia. As it is thus a law-term, "the people" would do much better to let it alone. But as it is a *long word*, the attempt to *make* them let it alone is something like trying to make a boy let a long stick of candy alone. As Hamlet says of "French falconers," they "fly *it* at anything they see," — appendages, ornaments, trappings; in short, a miscellaneous collection of any sort of things.

Not long ago, a remonstrance against a public procession on a Sunday, signed by a number of citizens, including many clergymen and other educated men, was published in the newspapers; and that remonstrance contained the word paraphernalia no less than three times, all in the same sense as this, —

"The employment of Sunday for public pageants, with bands of music and the *paraphernalia*, and noisy accompaniment, of a great procession," etc.

But what are paraphernalia? The word comes from the Greek, through the Latin, with very little change of spelling or pronunciation, and its meaning is, simply and concisely, *beyond dower;* independent of dower; that is, over and above dower; and, when combined in Law-Latin thus, *parapher nalia bona*, it means "*goods* in the wife's disposal," — "*articles* which a wife brings with her at her marriage, beyond her dower or jointure."

Those "articles," or "goods," may happen to consist of ornaments and appendages in the way of female finery; and they may not. The word refers to the *tenure*, and not to the *nature*, of the property. The articles are paraphernalia, not because they are — *if* they are — ornaments and appendages, but because they are articles of a wife's property, apart from her dower.

How absurd is it, then, to apply the word to the appendages of a public procession!

ALTERNATIVE.

This word means a choice — *one* choice — between two things. Yet popular usage has so corrupted it, that it is now commonly applied to the things themselves, and not to the choice between them; as thus, "You may take *either* alternative"; "I was forced to choose between *two* alternatives." And, indeed, some people go so far as to say "*several* alternatives were presented to him."

Nevertheless, if the primary meaning is respected, there can be but *one* alternative in any one case. *Two* alternatives is a contradiction in terms.

OUR MUTUAL FRIEND.

This is, so to speak, one of the approved **vulgarisms** of the day; and, notwithstanding the numberless exposures of its vulgarity, in newspapers, reviews, and elsewhere, it continues to flourish and increase. Apparently, nothing can stop it.

There is no ambiguity or uncertainty about the definition of "mutual." The lexicographers all agree upon it. It means simply, *reciprocal, interchanged;* whence anybody can see that it may apply to *actions* only and not to *things;* or, to speak more precisely, not to *living* things, or persons.

The actions may be mental or physical,—of the mind or of the body. People may reciprocally, interchangeably, mutually, love, hate, admire, etc. Or, they may reciprocally, etc. strike each other. Passions, sentiments, affections, actions, may be reciprocal, or mutual; but the actors, the persons themselves, cannot be so. *Friendship* may be mutual; but not the *friends.* Is not that plain?

But for all that, the person who reads this page, and turns from the page to a newspaper, will probably find "our mutual friend" in plain, unblushing typography! *

---

* Dickens has assumed a very unenviable responsibility in the matter of "mutual friend." He not only frequently uses the phrase in his writings, but he has published a novel bearing the title of "Our Mutual Friend," when any other title would have answered his purpose. Indeed, the title bears no relation whatever to the story. This is a defiance of public opinion, for which no apology could be offered.

There is a show of defence for Dickens in his pronunciation of

OVER HIS SIGNATURE.

No well-educated man could have originated such a preposterous conceit as the phrase "*over* his signature"; yet many well-educated men permit themselves to follow the example, that ignorance has placed before them; and if usage could sanction so stupid a blunder, the phrase would soon become good English.

The words *under* and *over* have various meanings, besides the designation of mere locality.

The terms "under oath," "under hand and seal," "under arms," "under compulsion," "under the sanction of," "under his own hand," "under his own signature," and so on, are fully established and authorized *forms* of expression; which have nothing to do with the *relative positions* of the persons and things indicated: they are *idiomatic*.

Yet, one or more of those "*persons* who come to town every day," will every day, for all time to come, announce that —

Whereas mankind have hitherto innocently used the phrase "*under* his own signature," in innocent unconsciousness that the *signature* is at the *bottom* of the instrument signed, they — mankind — will take note that nothing can be *under* a thing when

---

'*umble*, — that is, in his attempting to put the stamp of vulgarity on that pronunciation; because, however indefensible *humble* may be, — and that point will be fully considered in a subsequent part of this volume, — at least there are "two sides to the question." But no philologist defends, or attempts to defend, "our mutual friend."

it is over it, — nothing can be *under* that which is itself *under everything;* and that the said expression should be changed to "*over* his signature"; for the plain reason that the contents of the instrument *precede,* and *stand above,* to wit, *over,* the name at the bottom. That is conclusive, because there is no arguing against facts.

But the proclaimer of that rule should follow it to its consequences. He should further declare that "under seal" is just as disastrous an error as its predecessor, because the seal is also at the bottom. Furthermore, "under arms" cannot be correct, because a soldier when under arms is *not* under arms: *that* never happens until he is buried with his musket or his sword across his breast. "Under oath" is equally heretical, because the oath is mere breath; which, being exhaled, is *around* the witness, not *over* him. And finally, "under compulsion" *may* be right; but it cannot be proved so, until the relative positions of the man and the compulsion shall have been satisfactorily ascertained.

EPITHET.

Many men who are well educated, and many who are not so, strangely misunderstand this word. The shortest way to deal with it, is to refer to a dictionary. Worcester says,

"*Epithet,* an adjective denoting any quality, good or bad; a term expressing an attribute or quality."

That is to say, no part of speech other than an adjective is an epithet, and the import of an epithet is either good or bad.

Yet a large portion of all those persons, who speak or write the English language, would call the words *coward, thief, villain, fool, scoundrel,* etc., etc., " epithets."

Nor is that all. Very few people of a certain class can be made to understand, that while *adjectives,* only, are epithets; as *vile, cowardly, foolish,* etc., yet *good, just, honest, handsome,* etc., are also epithets. The popular impression is, that to " apply epithets " to a person, is to vilify and insult him.

" LOOKED BEAUTIFULLY."

A deal of argument has been expended on the question whether an adjective is more proper than an adverb in such phrases as " the trees looked magnificently," " the clouds looked splendidly," " the water looked frightfully," " Miss Smith looked beautifully," etc.

But there is little room, or occasion, for argument in the case. Whatever there is of doubt about it, arises from a misapprehension of the meaning of the verb *to look,* in that phraseology. It there has its strictly neuter meaning of *seeming.*

As there used, it does not mean the *act of looking with* the eye, but the *fact of appearing to* the eye: and all question about the accuracy of the phrases will disappear the moment the right meaning is made plain by a substituted word.

The speaker, in such cases, means that the persons, or things, spoken of *are*, or *seem*, or *appear* magnificent, beautiful, etc. No one would think of saying that " the clouds *are magnificently*."

It is perhaps unnecessary to add that adverbs refer to, or qualify, what a person or thing *does;* and adjectives, what a person or thing *is*, or *seems* to be.

AT LENGTH.

The phrase *at length* is often used in the place of *at last*, but that is not its meaning.

" I have heard from my friend *at length*," means that I have heard fully and in detail: a *long* statement, or letter.

To hear from him *at last*, is to hear from him after a long delay.

DISTINGUISH DISCRIMINATE.

"Distinguish" is often used for "discriminate"; as, " I could not distinguish between them."

There is a great array of precedent for this; but any one who is sensitive to niceties in language must see the advantage of *discriminating* between the two words.

"Distinguish" has other and distinct meanings; and its force as to them is weakened by the imposing on it of too many duties. The fact, that " discriminate " retains its originally limited signification, shows the advantages of such retention, and should be a hint to those persons who are addicted to seeking substitutes.

CURIOUS.

A correspondent of the *London Athenæum*, March, 1866, says: —

"By newspaper writers, and even by those who may be looked upon as authorities, this word is now employed as quite equivalent to *strange* or *remarkable*.

"Nothing is more common than to read in the daily prints of *curious coincidences*. On every page, we meet with some paragraphs beginning, *it is a curious fact*. Or, we may even read such a sentence as this: *The Emperor himself was present, but, curiously enough, he asked no questions!*

"This use of the word is at once novel and absurd; and, I cannot but think, unknown in the writings of every good author. The word, as it has hitherto been employed by correct writers, has two meanings, akin to each other, differing a little, but both very distinct from that of *strange*, or *extraordinary*.

"It was primarily applied only to persons, bearing the meaning of *prying* or *inquisitive;* only *curious*, unlike those words, does not imply anything of moral blame. Curious men (more usually, *the curious*), as Addison wrote of them, were simply those who intermeddled with all knowledge.

"But it is also, with sufficient sanction, applied to things. When so applied, it means very nice, or intricate; e. g. an elaborate, delicate piece of stone or ivory work might be described as *curiously* carved.

"To use the word otherwise than in these senses is a wilful abuse of language. We have *remarkable, strange, queer*, and a host of other words perfectly fitted to fill the place, into which so many people are trying to push poor *curious*."

PECULIAR.

"Peculiar" and "peculiarly" have nearly lost their force and their *peculiarity* of signification, by having become used interchangeably with *extremely, intensely, superlatively*, etc.; although the noun, *peculiarity*, substantially holds its original position. In this case, as in the case of "distinguish," they lose much of the force of their precision, by being perverted from their strict sense.

MOST.

Everybody abuses this word. At least, nobody, with less patience and perseverance than Diogenes, can find an author who is innocent of such abuse.

Most is the superlative of *much*; and also, secondarily, of *many*; but, as to many other English words, usage has given it a third duty to perform and a second and subordinate sense to carry; which duty it performs indifferently, and not without injury to itself: for the perversion detracts from its original force. This secondary sense is nearly, if not exactly, the equivalent of *very*, a word that falls entirely short of being superlative; and the constant use of "most" in that sense necessarily weakens its force in *any* sense.

Indeed, that effect directly follows that cause; as is seen in the fact that good writers have, for a century or two, fallen into a habit of using "most" in its original and superlative sense, yet applying it to adjectives or adverbs that are already, either technically or intrinsically, superlative of themselves; or, they prefix it to a verb that expresses superlative action: either of which uses is tautological, superfluous, and impertinent. These remarks will be best illustrated by citations, in some of which the word is used in its primary, and in others in its secondary, sense.

MILTON says,
"If what is urged
Main reason to persuade immediate war
Did not dissuade me most, and seem to cast
Ominous conjecture on the whole success;
When he who *most* excels in fact of arms,
In what he counsels and in what excels," etc.

SHAKESPEARE says,
"*Most* potent, grave, and reverend seignors,
My very noble and approved good masters,
That I have ta'en away this old man's daughter,
It is *most true;* true, I have married her," etc

JOHNSON says,
"It is the sage advice of Epictetus that a man should accustom himself often to think of what is *most* shocking and terrible, that, by such reflections, he may be preserved from," etc.

ADDISON says,
"I had not been long at the university before I distinguished myself by a *most* profound silence."

Horace Walpole says,

"I have considered your suggestions as to so and so; it is a *most just* idea."

Burke says,

"If this system has so ill answered its own grand pretence of saving the king from employing persons disagreeable to him, has it given more peace and tranquillity to his majesty's private hours? No, *most certainly.*"

Chesterfield says,

"He was a *most complete* orator and debater in the House of Commons."

Littleton says,

"This was *most* extraordinary virtue in one who has lived amid all the license of camps," etc.

Smollett says,

"He was doubtless an object of *most perfect* esteem and admiration," etc.

Goldsmith says,

"Yet, even in these, the reader's memory may possibly suggest the names of some, whose works, still preserved, discover a *most* extensive erudition."

Washington Irving says,

"His affections were so social and generous, that when he had money, he gave it *most* liberally away."

Prescott says,

"If I have reserved his name for the last, in the list of those to whose good offices I am indebted, it is, *most* assuredly, not because I value his services least."

Daniel Webster says,

"But, soon afterward, having reason to suspect that Columbia and Mexico were preparing to attack Cuba, and knowing that such an event would *most* seriously affect us," etc.

Edward Everett says,

"It requires little argument to show, that such a system must *most* widely and *most* powerfully have the effect of appealing to whatever of energy the land contains."

Here follow certain random selections from the newspapers: —

"Though the effort be earnest, the coin is base, and it is *most effectually* nailed to the counter in the short article we have," etc.

"We will not say that Paulding has no faults as a writer; but it is *most undeniable* that, for every one of his faults, a careful critic might produce," etc.

"The brilliancy of Andrew Jackson's military career is *most unalterably* certified by," etc.

"It is a *most* melancholy and *most unaccountable* fact, that some hundreds of deluded individuals have given in their adherence," etc.

"He began in early life as a writer; and, after forty years' labor, he accomplished a *most* extensive and valuable collection," etc.

"This picture is a real gem, and a *most undoubted* original."

It is needless to prolong this list of quotations. They might be extended to many thousands. But what is worthy of special notice is the fact that they are not selected from others in any one work of their authors. In each instance, the first *most* that was found in a volume is the one here quoted. And yet, the reader will see that, in almost every case, the sentence would be improved by the omission of the word *most*.

The passages from Milton and Shakespeare, being poetry, could not be so abridged, unless another word were substituted; but that fact is immaterial to the argument.

What is true of the foregoing extracts is equally true of the pages of English literature generally. That is to say, if a man would cross out "most" wherever he can find it in any book in the English language, he would in *al*most every instance improve the style of the book.

And, on the other hand, if good writers had, in time past, adhered to the conservative principle of avoiding the free use of certain words in a secondary sense, they would have done much toward preserving the precision of our language.

THE REVEREND.

The omission of the definite article before the words "honourable" and "reverend," when one speaks of persons entitled to those epithets, has become very common of late; but the author of this book is not aware of anybody's having assigned a reason for the omission. Its propriety may be tried by the process of illustration. Admit, for the sake of argument, that adjectives do not, when so used, require the article, or any prefixed word; and then see how its omission affects this paragraph:—

At last annual meeting of Blank Book Society, honourable John Smith took the chair, assisted by reverend John Brown and venerable John White. The office of secretary would have been filled by late John Green, but for his decease, which rendered him ineligible. His place was supplied by inevitable John Black. In the course of the evening, eulogiums were pronounced on distinguished John Gray, and notorious Joseph Brown. Marked compliment was also paid to able historian Joseph White, discriminating philosopher Joseph Green, and learned professor Joseph Black. But conspicuous speech of the evening was witty Joseph Gray's apostrophe to eminent astronomer Jacob Brown, subtle logician Jacob White, and sound mathematician Jacob Green. His reference to learned Jacob Black was a brilliant hit. Profound metaphysician Jacob Gray was not forgotten, and indefatigable traveller Peter Brown was remembered by a good anecdote. Clever artist Peter Gray was, in fact, only celebrity omitted.

THE BOOK GENESIS.

The omission of the preposition *of*, which has recently been practised in the American pulpit, is thus treated by Dean Alford in the "Queen's English," in reference to the *Queen's* clergymen:—

"There is a piece of affectation becoming sadly

common among our younger clergy; namely, the omission of *of* in proclaiming from the desk *Here beginneth the first chapter of the book Genesis*, etc.

"I believe the excuse, if it can be called one, set up for this violation of usage is, that the *Book of Genesis* and the *Book of Daniel* cannot both be right, because the former was not written by Genesis, as the latter was by Daniel. But this simply betrays ignorance of the meaning of the preposition *of*. It is used to denote authorship; as the Book of Daniel: to denote subject-matter; as the First Book of Kings: and as a note of apposition signifying *which is called;* as the book of Genesis, of Exodus, etc.

"The pedant, who ignores *of* in the reading-desk, must however, to be consistent, omit it elsewhere: *I left the city London, and passed through county Kent, leaving realm England at town Dover,*" etc.

WIDOW LADY.

Widow-*lady* and widow-*woman* are frequently encountered in conversation and in print. But whether either of them has yet been encountered *by* a widower-*gentleman* or a widower-*man*, remains to be discovered.

ONE.

One, when used as a pronoun in the singular number, is a very convenient and useful word; as,

"Two opportunities presented themselves, and he, fortunately, chose the right *one*.

"There were several swords on the table, but I had the luck to take the best *one* of all."

But when the word is used in the plural, although such use is grammatically correct, the effect is grotesque; as,

"Of the books he sent, I found three very good *ones*, but the remainder were particularly dull."

Omit the "very good" in the first branch of that sentence, and the odd expression, *three ones*, remains.

BUT THAT.

But that, when the two words are used together and each is used as a conjunction, seems to be a favorite combination with some writers; and good writers do not always escape it.

The phrase is bad enough in itself; and is worse in view of its consequence; namely, the misleading of other people into the lower vulgarism of *but what;* as in the genial reply of Mr. Jobling (*né Weevle*) of Bleak House: —

"Thank you, Guppy, I don't know *but what* I will take a marrow pudding."

The Joblings of society must of course be left where Dickens places them; but it is desirable for educated men to set a better example than SOUTHEY did, when he wrote,

"There can be no question *but that* both the language and the characters are Hebrew."

And even that is not quite so bad as a line of TRENCH, in his book on this very subject of good English, — "English Past and Present": —

"He never doubts *but that* he knows their intentions";
because SOUTHEY was writing a work of fiction,— "The Doctor,"— and was not necessarily on his guard: "not *but what* he should have been," however, as Mr. Jobling might say.

THAT, IN THAT, ETC.

Many writers have a habit of *omitting* "that," from what would seem to be a propensity to over-neatness of style; or, it may be omitted through carelessness. The omission makes a sentence both inaccurate and inelegant. Precision is always an element of a finished style. These are instances of the omission:—

"It was a long time before I ascertained [that] I had lost the book." "We all know [that] history constantly reproduces itself." "He assured me [that] the fact was otherwise." "Those who are competent to judge say [that] he will never succeed." And so on, indefinitely.

Again, "that" is frequently used by some good, and by all poor, writers in a phrase that is only one remove from slang. Even Trench uses it. He says ("English Past and Present"): "It is undoubtedly becoming different from what it has been, but only different [this should be *different only*] in that it is passing into another stage of its development."

Here *in that* means nothing less than in *this respect, that*, which is a very unreasonable burden for so short a word — to say nothing of the vulgarism of the phrase. It is making "that" do double duty,— as a pronoun and a conjunction.

Trench also says, in the same volume, "I cannot think *but that* this is stated too strongly." Which is not only, as Polonius says, "a vile phrase," but it fails to express the meaning of the writer. He means, "I cannot *but think that*," etc. In other words, he *says* he *cannot think*, and he *means* he *cannot help thinking*.

It is not overstating the case to say that Dean Trench, while he is beyond question a writer of general elegance and force, is frequently guilty of extreme carelessness,— which, in books of philological criticism, is hardly to be excused. In addition to his already-cited blunders, here is a sentence which, within the compass of fifteen lines, contains four blunders,— namely, two errors and two inelegancies : "It can be regarded in no *other* light *but* as a riddle which no one has succeeded in solving. . . . . *Had* they *had* their rise first in books, *then* it would be easily traced; had it been from the schools of the learned, these would not *have failed* to *have left* a recognizable stamp and mark upon them."

The "but" should be *than;* the "then" should be omitted; and "have left" should be *leave.*

IN SO FAR AS.

This is a variation of "in that"; the chief difference between the two being that, while one of the phrases has too few words, the other has too many.

As to frequency of use, they are nearly equal. These are instances: —

"We are to act up to the extent of our knowledge; but, *in so far as* our knowledge falls short," etc.

"A want of proper opportunity would suffice, *in so far as* the want could be shown."

It seems strange that so clumsy a phrase could get into use, when the proper phrase is so familiar and simple; but so it is that men will cumber themselves about many things when but few things are needed. The *in* of the phrase in question is worse than superfluous. It might with equal propriety be added to this, or any similar, sentence: —

"He was much emaciated, *in* so much so, indeed, that no one recognized him"; or, "she is beautiful, *in* so beautiful, that every man falls in love with her."

CORRESPOND.

The verb *to correspond* has two meanings: one, to be adapted to, or appropriate to, etc., when it always requires the preposition *to* after it; as,

"His style of living corresponded *to* his means";

"The style of its architecture corresponded *to* the size of the square";

and the other, to hold, or have, intercourse by letters; in which sense it requires the preposition *with;* as,

"I have corresponded *with* him for years."

But the majority of writers, good and bad, use *with* in both cases.

WITHOUT.

Almost everybody uses this word as the synonyme of *unless:* "I would not do it *without* he consented," and so on. But such a use of the word is entirely unjustifiable.

STOPPING.

It is a matter of almost daily experience to find in the newspapers sentences like this, —

"General Grant and his family have arrived in town, and are *stopping* at the Fifth Avenue Hotel."

On reading such an announcement, one is tempted to inquire, —

"When will General Grant *stop* 'stopping'?"

Stopping is not a continuous process, like *going, living*, etc. To stop is to do a single act that terminates the prior action. The act may be repeated, but it cannot be continued.*

PEN.

Bulwer, in his play of Richelieu, had the good fortune to do, what few men can hope to do: he wrote a line that is likely to live for ages. The great Cardinal says,

> "Beneath the rule of men entirely great,
> The pen is mightier than the sword."

That, however, was written a quarter of a century ago, when the *full* power of the pen was not developed. Were Bulwer to write his play now,

---

* The man who did *not* invite his (so-called) friend to visit him, understood the meaning of words when he said, "If you come, at any time, within ten miles of my house, just *stop*."

with the light which the gentlemen of the newspapers have thrown on the subject, he would probably change his immortal line to,

"The pen is mightier than the *man*."

Because, when Bulwer wrote that play, he *did* write it; whereas the present newspaper account of the transaction would be that "The new play of Richelieu is attributed to *the pen* of Bulwer."

OF ALL OTHERS.

Criticism has almost exhausted itself in exhibiting the absurdity of this phrase: but nobody gives heed to the criticisms. Like "our mutual friend," the more it is criticised, the more people use it. Books, newspapers, and conversation overflow with it.

It is forced into all varieties of sentences, of which any one or two will suffice as examples: —

"That style of warfare is, *of all others*, the most barbarous."

"A stain *of all others* the most difficult to expunge."

How one thing can be *of other* things, is the question. One thing can be *above* other things, but it cannot be *of* them. A thing can be *of all things, the most*; or, *of all things, the richest*, etc., or, of *a class*, the best; but the introduction of " others " into the phrases in question *excludes* from the " class," or from the " all," the very thing named.

The two sentences above quoted should be changed by the substitution of *above* for " of "; or, by changing "others" to *styles* and *stains*, respectively.

A HEARTY MEAL.

This phrase is appropriated chiefly by the novelists; who, alone, have much occasion for it. Dickens "seriously inclines" to it, although generally he writes the purest English of the whole fraternity; always excepting Anthony Trollope, and the anonymous author of a recently published story called "Tony Butler." Tony Butler is the work of a master, whoever he may be.

As to the "hearty meal," it is, no doubt, very acceptable to the personage in the book who eats it; it is doubtless "quite to his *taste*"; but preserve us from the taste of the man who writes it!

IN OUR MIDST.

This is a common phrase in sermons, homilies, and religious newspapers; and it is not uncommon elsewhere.

Quaint forms of expression, in the treating of religious and moral subjects, have become familiar, and are felt to be appropriate, because our translation of the Bible is full of them. But quaintness must not take the place of accuracy in language: besides, though the phrase in question may be traced to the Bible, it cannot be found in the Bible.

Midst means, simply, *middle*, and it means nothing else; hence, "in our midst" is no better than *in our middle*.

Again, "midst" is not an absolute, or independent, term. It must be used in connection with some other word, or preceded by the definite article; indeed, the article is indispensable. We have "in the midst" in the Bible, *midst* being there used as one of the parts of a locality, previously indicated. But the more usual form of its correct use requires not only the definite article before it, but the preposition *of* after it; as, *in the midst of* a storm, or the confusion, or the discussion, etc.

Webster's last Dictionary has the following comments: —

"The phrase *in our midst* has, unhappily, gained great currency in this country, and it is sometimes, though rarely, to be found in the writings of respectable English authors. The expression seems contrary to the genius of the language, as well as opposed to the practice of our best and most accurate writers, and should therefore be abandoned."

Moreover, here, as elsewhere, the advocates of a phrase must abide its consequences. If "in our midst" is tolerated, who can prevent the next step in the innovation; namely, "our *little* midst"?

YOU ARE MISTAKEN.

This phrase, as popularly used, is one of the most widely disseminated of philological errors.

The verb *to mistake* is a compound of *mis* and *take;* and it means simply to *take amiss*, to take erroneously.

The "take" of the combination has two significations,—taking physically and taking mentally; that is, to take by or with the hand, and by or with the mind. The word *mistake* is seldom, perhaps never, used in the former sense. In the latter sense, it may be defined by the verbs *misjudge, misconceive, misapprehend, misunderstand*.

Therefore, to say that a person *mistakes* the facts of a case, or the acts, opinions, intentions, or words of another person, is equivalent to saying that he misjudges, misconceives, misapprehends, or misunderstands them.

And, on the other hand, to say "you are mistaken," in regard to the acts, facts, opinions, etc., is equivalent to saying *you are misjudged*, misconceived, misapprehended, misunderstood, thereabout.

But, as the phrase is commonly used, *that* is exactly what the speaker does not mean. He *intends* to tell his friend that *he* (the friend) is wrong, or in error; but he *says* that he is himself in error.

For example, A says to B, "The Central Park is ten miles long." B replies, "You are mistaken; it is only three miles long."

In that case, A is *not* mistaken, because he is not misunderstood by B. He *mistook* the fact, and that is what B should have said,—"You mistake."

Again, A says to B, "Dr. Brown has become unsound in his theology; he said so and so." B replies, "You are mistaken; he said so and so."

Here again A is not *mistaken;* he *mistook*, he misapprehended, etc., the Doctor's words or his meaning.

In short, whenever A wishes to tell B that he is wrong, or in error, in a remark like those here cited, he should say " you mistake," or " you are wrong," and not " you are mistaken."

As to the noun, " mistake." Analogically, *a mistake* seems to be little better than a *misjudge*, a *misconceive*, a *misapprehend*, a *misunderstand;* and quite as bad as an *undertake*, or an *overtake*. And those words, ridiculous as they appear, need not be scouted as impossible applicants for admission into the language; so long as everybody knows that, among ignorant people, " a recommend " is a common substitute for a *recommendation;* and " an invite," for an *invitation*. Furthermore, we have the exact equivalent of " recommend " and " invite," already adopted and in daily use in one of the "learned professions." Hardly a case is tried in our courts of law, in the progress of which trial papers are not introduced that are called and marked " *exhibits*." And our custom-house daily grants its "*permits*" for the discharge of merchandise from vessels and warehouses.

Hence, as most of our philological vulgarisms originate with illiterate people, and gradually rise in the popular current until, at last, they are adopted by good writers, — a *recommend*, an *invite*, an *overtake*, and *any other* words, *may* become good English, on the theory that *usage* is the end of the law. Besides, there is this additional difficulty about the noun *mistake*, when used as the equivalent of *an error*, — that it tends strongly toward sanctioning the misuse of the verb, as already discussed. For, when we become accustomed to the use of " a mistake," it seems inconsistent to deny that " you are mistaken " and " you are in error " are interchangeable terms.

When one has in mind the true meaning of the verb, what a confusing jumble of thought ensues from hearing the phrase, " You *made a mistake*," — as if one should say, " You *made a misunderstand!*"

However, these comments on the *noun* mistake are intended to be speculative, rather than critical; for whether the noun is well or ill formed, and whether or not its use tends to accredit the verb in a wrong sense, neither its formation nor its use can now be disturbed. The word is too firmly rooted in the language, to be subject to serious criticism.

COMPARATIVE ADJECTIVES.

Comparative adjectives, as *wiser*, *better*, *larger*, etc., etc., and also the contrasting adjectives, *different*, *other*, etc., are very often inelegantly used by being misplaced; as,

" That is a much *better* statement of the case *than* yours."

" Yours is a *larger* plot of ground *than* John's."

" This is a *different* course of proceeding *from* what I expected."

" I could take no *other* method of silencing him *than* the one I took."

Those sentences should be thus altered:

" That statement of the case is much *better than* yours."

"Your plot of ground is *larger than* John's."

"That course of proceeding is *different from* what I expected."

"I could take no method of silencing him, *other than* the one I took."

The fault, in such cases, is a fault of *construction*, or *position*, — separating the adjective from the conjunction. As a rule, they should be brought together; and when the reader sees the two forms side by side, he needs no argument to show him the advantage of bringing them together.

Very few writers seem to understand this; or, at least, very few writers take the trouble to avoid the error; for the instances of the error, in every department of literature, may be counted by tens of thousands.

Mr. Marsh, in his series of criticisms on Webster's Dictionary published in *The Nation*, permits himself to write the following formidable specimen of this fault of construction (*The Nation*, September 20th): —

"In like manner, false derivations of *buoy, camlet*, and hundreds of other words, are almost universally adopted, because lexicographers have found it *easier* to imagine a connection between vocables so like each other as *boja*, a fetter or chain, and *buoy; camel* and *camlet; than* to search out the actual history of the derivatives in question."

How *easy* would it have been for Mr. Marsh to say, — "lexicographers have found *that* to imagine a connection .... *is easier than* to search out," etc.

Mr. Marsh, in the same paper, says, "*Neither* the history, the form, nor the meaning of a word," — thus applying "neither" to *three* objects. But, *per contra*, he gives, in the same paragraph, the following able and perspicuous criticism on one of Webster's etymologies: —

"In a dictionary on the plan of that before us there must also be a limit to the amount of collateral etymological illustration, and space is occupied which might be better employed whenever facts are stated which serve to explain neither the history, the form, nor the meaning of a word. The former editions of Webster were very extravagant in this respect, and though the revisers have, in most cases, retrenched such superfluities, they have sometimes, from inadvertence, no doubt, rather than deliberate intention, suffered them to remain. Thus, the etymology of *profession* refers us to the French *profession*, the Provençal *professio*, the Spanish *profesion*, the Italian *professione*, and the Latin *professio*. Now the French word is important, because it accounts for the form of the English, the Latin because it gives us the proximate source of the French; the other three explain nothing whatever, and are of no more use or instruction to the English student than totally unrelated Russian, Hungarian, or Turkish equivalents of the same word would be."

This is a quiet, but rather sharp, comment on the former claim of Webster's publishers, — that his dictionary was superior to all others by reason of, and in proportion to, the voluminousness of its etymologies.

THE INFINITIVE MOOD.

The use of a verb — any verb — in the past tense, with an infinitive in the past tense, is another of the blunders that may be found on almost every page of English literature. It is even more common than "of all others"; although, like that, it has been perseveringly criticised for many years.

Johnson says,

"Had this been the fate of Tasso, he would have been able *to have celebrated* the condescension of your majesty in noble language."

Southey says,

"Gray might perhaps have been able *to have rendered* him more temperate in his political views."

Wilson says,

"Byron's modesty was shocked at the sight of waltzing, which he would not have suffered the Guiccioli *to have indulged* in, even with her own husband."

Jeffrey says,

"Swift, but a few months before, was willing *to have hazarded* all the horrors of civil war."

Alison says,

"It was expected that his first act *would have been to have sent* for Lords Grey and Grenville." *

Trench says,

"Those who would gladly have seen the Anglo

---

* This sentence contains a double blunder: but that is nothing uncommon for Alison.

Saxon *to have predominated* over the Latin element in our language."

The infinitives in the foregoing quotations should be, severally, *to celebrate, to render, to indulge, to hazard, would be to send;* while Trench's sentence should be, " *the Anglo-Saxon predominate.*"

When such writers set such examples, who can wonder that all subsequent writers follow them?

The present infinitive, though often misused, is so used much less frequently than the past. Besides, the error can be much more briefly explained.

The present infinitive consists of the particle *to* and the verb; as, *to speak.* But, grammatically, the particle is a *part* of the verb, and a part inseparable from it, as much so as is any other mere prefix. Indeed, as much so as a prefixed syllable that makes a compound word, as *in* and *separable*, in the word *inseparable*. But some person who happened to hear, or see, a forcible expression made by placing an adverb between an auxiliary and its principal verb — which is a very different case from this case — wished, probably, to do likewise with the infinitive; and he placed *his* adverb between the particle and the verb. An abundance of followers was found " *to* immediately *imitate*" the preposterous example, which is as notable for its pedantry as for its ignorance.

SHOULD HAVE REGRETTED HIS HAVING BEEN, ETC.

Akin to this use of the past, for the present, infinitive, is a compound of past tenses involved in a phrase like this: "I should have regretted his having been killed." In this case, if the speaker means that he *would once have regretted* what, for reasons, he does not now regret, he should say, "I should have regretted his *being* killed"; but if he means that he "*would now* regret," etc., he ought to say, "I should regret his having been killed." In short, *one* branch of the sentence must refer to the present time.

Trench says, in "English Past and Present," "A lover of his native tongue will tremble to think what that tongue *would have become*, if all the vocables from the Latin and Greek . . . . *had been admitted* . . . . and if . . . . *had* not *been rejected*," etc.

Obviously, this should be, "what the tongue *would be*, if so and so *had been*"; because, how could a lover of his native tongue tremble at a danger, or an evil, that is *past?*

THE POSSESSIVE CASE.

There seems to be a difference of opinion, even among philologists, about the accuracy of sentences like these: —

"The reason of the king not giving his consent, has at last been divulged."

"The doctor insisted on John being bled."

"He would not be satisfied without the major throwing it away."

"The best apology for the governor signing the paper, is," etc.

Dean Alford says on this point: —

"A correspondent inquires respecting the correctness of such sentences as the following : Day and night are a consequence* of the earth revolving on its axis. He maintains † that, here, *revolving* is a verbal noun, equivalent to *revolution;* and that we ought to say, — a consequence of the *earth's* revolving on its axis. He believes he has proved this, by the test of substituting the pronoun for 'earth': Day and night are a consequence of *its* revolving on its axis, — where, he rightly says, no one would think of saying *it* revolving. At first sight, this appears decisive. But, let us examine a little

---

* One would suppose that the Dean might as well have rebuked his correspondent for writing "a consequence" instead of *consequences.*

† This word is of questionable propriety in the circumstances. A critic should avoid doubtful words. The primary meaning of "maintain" involves a *successful* upholding, which success the Dean proceeds in this case to *deny.*

A man once said to his friend, at the end of a discussion, "I *maintain* my opinion, for all that." "Excuse me," was the rejoinder; "you *retain* your opinion."

Again, the Dean says, " the use of *here lies the remains of* has been *justified* by a correspondent on such and such grounds "; after which, he proceeds to say, in the same paragraph, that "the *defence* of his correspondent is unquestionably wrong. How, then could the correspondent have "justified" the phrase ?

It so happens, that the Dean furnishes a commentary on a precisely similar misuse of a word, in his paragraph 346. He is speaking of the misuse of *sustain.* "To sustain means to *endure,* to *bear up under;* but to sustain a bereavement "— that is the phrase he criticises — "does not properly mean to undergo or suffer a loss, but to behave bravely under it. In the newspapers, however, 'sustain' comes in for the happening to men of all the ills and accidents possible."

further. It is somewhat curious,* that in this last sentence we may leave out the possessive pronoun without obscuring the sense : thus, Our earth enjoys day and night as a consequence of revolving on its axis," etc.

That is strange reasoning. The sentence which the Dean offers as an illustration is entirely different from the sentence he professes to illustrate : and thus, though *his* sentence is correct, its correctness does not prove the other incorrect.

The test of substituting the pronoun is good. The Dean says it " at first sight appears decisive " : which is true. And, moreover, it *is* decisive at first sight, and at second sight, and at *any* " sight."

Does the Dean seriously mean to say that, in a given sentence, a noun does not require the possessive case, when a substituted pronoun does require it? Do the principles of grammatical government *vary* between a noun and a pronoun ?

Let us look at the four quoted sentences at the beginning of this section on the Possessive Case ; and reproduce them in the three positions, — with and without the possessive of the noun, and with the pronoun : —

The reason of the *king* (*king's*) (*his*) not giving his consent has at last been divulged ;

The doctor insisted on *John* (*John's*) (*his*) being bled ;

He would not be satisfied without the *major* (*major's*) (*his*) throwing it away ;

* *See* page 51.

The best apology for the *governor* (*governor's*) (*his*) signing the paper, is, etc.

Of course in all but the second quotation the *the* before the questionable noun must be omitted when the pronoun is used.

Now, take the *actual* equivalent of the correspondent's own sentence with such variations as shall try its grammar without changing its syntax: —

Disease and death are consequences of the *man* neglecting the doctor's advice;

Disease and death are consequences of *me* neglecting the doctor's advice;

Disease and death are consequences of *he*, or *him*, neglecting the doctor's advice.

Can any person doubt that the possessive case is indispensable in those instances?

A late number of the *London Times* has this sentence: —

"The solution could *only* be put off either by the Emperor *Napoleon* resolving on a prolonged occupation of Mexico, or by the Emperor *Maximilian* being able to reply," etc.

The almost universal misuse, by the misplacing, of the word *only* will be considered on a subsequent page; but a few words here may not be amiss. Strictly speaking, that sentence is so arranged that instead of *only's* being misplaced, one should say that there is no place for it.

It means, as the preceding lines of the paragraph would show if they were here quoted, that the suggested action of one or the other of the emperors is *the only way* to postpone the solution. Therefore, its place in the quoted sentence *would* be this: " The solution could be put off *only either by* the Emperor Napoleon," etc., which is altogether too outrageous to be thought of; hence, " only " has no place and must be stricken out.

But the sentence from the *Times* is a recent and responsible instance of the omission of the possessive case. The Dean would say that the sentence is correct, but the Dean would be wrong. " Napoleon " and " Maximilian " should be *Napoleon's* and *Maximilian's*.

The *reason* for the necessity of the possessive case in such sentences is to be found in the meaning of the words: the solution is to be put off— *if* put off—by *Napoleon's act;* to wit, *his* resolving so and so: or, by *Maximilian's act;* that is, *his* " being able " so and so. Dean Alford's argument virtually assumes that Napoleon and Maximilian are in the objective case, and are governed by the preposition *by*, which is contradicted by the sense of the passage. So, again, in the above-quoted sentence of the Dean, " Day and night are consequences of the *earth's act*, — to wit, *its* revolving on its axis ": the " consequences " are not the " consequences *of the earth*," but of the " revolving," and the *revolving* is the *earth's act:* it is the *earth's revolving* — which is the point at issue.

Jenkins and *Jones* have good reason to complain of the squeamishness that refuses them the privilege of a full possessive case, which, however, is freely accorded to *Brown* and *Smith*. On the same page that contains a tribute to Brown's high character, we find another tribute to Jenkins' memory.

Byron made short work of that, when he wrote,

> " And ere the faithless truce was broke
> Which freed her from the unchristian yoke,
> With him his gentle daughter came;
> Nor there since Menelaus's dame
> Forsook," etc.

In that case, the printer may do what he pleases with the final *s*, — use it, or omit it; but the reader will take care to pronounce it — if he knows how to read.

WHOSE.

Every man who is sensitive on the subject of correct language, must have felt the want of an impersonal relative pronoun, the possessive case of which should hold toward *things* the relation that " whose " holds to *persons*. But there is no such pronoun, and no human ingenuity can make one. In its absence, *whose* has been substituted as a matter of necessity and almost by common consent; as,

" We found in the grove one enormous tree *whose* height we estimated to be more than two hundred feet."

Some of the best English writers have used " whose " in this sense; Gibbon uses it frequently, and on the whole it should be accepted as inevitable.

But here, as elsewhere, there are dissenting votes.

Mr. Washington Moon, an expert English philologist, who is known as an able and persistent assailant of Dean Alford's book, has written several letters for the *Round Table*, in which he sharply criticises the *style* of Mr. Marsh's communications in *The Nation*, already mentioned. Mr. Moon thus stands in the position of a *critic criticising a criticising critic;* in which capacity *he* has not escaped criticism at the hands of third parties. Mr. Moon, speaking of Mr. Marsh's use of *whose* in the way above mentioned, says: —

— Can either the relative pronoun *who*, or its possessive *whose*, correctly be employed concerning inanimate objects? I think not. Of the relative pronouns, *who* and *whose* apply either to persons, or to things personified; *which* applies to irrational animals, to inanimate objects, and sometimes to infants; and *that* is used to prevent the too frequent repetitions of *who* and of *which*, and applies equally to persons, to animals, and to things. Such is our modern usage; and to it we ought to conform. I am aware that, in olden time, it was the custom to use *which* when speaking of persons; hence the phrase, "Our Father *which* art in heaven." It was the custom also to say *whose* when speaking of things; hence, in the opening lines of Paradise Lost we read —

"Of man's first disobedience, and the fruit
Of that forbidden tree *whose* mortal taste."

But now the best writers, when speaking of inanimate objects, use *of which* instead of *whose;* and I am surprised to find Mr. Marsh saying, "How can we define *that whose* being, whose action, whose conditions, whose limitations we cannot comprehend?" Would it not have been better to say, "How can we define that *of which* we cannot comprehend the being, the action, the conditions, the limitations?" —

Of which, in the first place, be it remarked, the assertion — "the best writers use *of which* instead of *whose*" — is *not true,* in the unqualified way here stated.

Of which, in the second place, be it remarked, the third sentence of Mr. Moon's paragraph is supererogatory.

And of which, in the third place, be it remarked, a man may have the best of an argument and yet be practically on the wrong side of the question argued.

The frequent use of *whose,* in the way cited, by many of the best writers, for the last hundred years, establishes a *prima facie* case of *necessity;* for so frequent a violation of so obvious a rule, could hardly have been accidental. *Whose* was so used because there was no help for it, — no substitute for it. Mr. Moon's suggested substitute is not new; nor does its grammatical accuracy help it to take, in all cases, the place he assigns to it. It therefore does not satisfy the necessity.

An innovation upon a philological principle is

one thing, and a violation of a philological rule is also one thing; neither of which can be justified in the abstract. And when either is made *without necessity*, it cannot be justified at all: as, for example, the fabrication of a word *that is not needed;* or, the misuse of a word or phrase that can easily be corrected. But an innovation upon a principle, or a violation of a rule, when either is done to satisfy a universally acknowledged necessity, is another thing.

In such a case, the plea of Bassanio to Portia,

"To do a great right, do a little wrong,"

comes with great force. It is true, Portia replies,

"It must not be;
'T would be recorded *for a precedent*":

and Justice could make no other response. But Portia, herself, says to Shylock,

"Though *justice* be thy plea, consider this,—
That in the course of justice, none of us
Should see salvation; we do pray for mercy;
And that same prayer should teach us all to render
The deeds of mercy."

That quotation, with *necessity* substituted for "mercy," is commended to Mr. Moon's notice.

JOURNAL.

This word comes to us directly from the French, without any change of spelling and with little change of pronunciation. The French *journal* is from the Latin *diurnalis*, whence, also, the English *diurnal*. This etymology renders the definition inevitable and — one would think — exclusive; namely, something pertaining to *daily* use; and hence its application to a *daily* newspaper is obviously proper.

But, by a strange latitude of application, the word has finally come to be used for a weekly newspaper and even for a quarterly review. The writers for the English Quarterlies, who certainly rank high as "*good* writers," frequently refer, in speaking of themselves, " to the course uniformly pursued by this journal."

UNIVERSE.

The word *universe* is very often used as the mere synonyme of *world*, this world, the earth; when a writer, or speaker, wishes to give *emphasis* to an assertion; as,

" There is not a *man* in the *universe* who could do it."

" That is the finest *ship* in the *universe*."

" No *army* in the *universe* could beat them."

No doubt, there is a universe; but the word means *all* created things, as a whole; not only our entire solar system, but all the other systems of which the fixed stars are but the centres.

Therefore, to use the word as meaning merely the earth — which is necessarily involved by peopling or occupying it with things earthly — is absurd; not to say, that it conveys an impression of the ignorance of the meaning of the word, on the part of the writer or speaker.

RIDE. DRIVE.

The use of *drive*, for *ride*, to express being conveyed in a carriage instead of on a horse, is a miserable affectation of accuracy. There is no accuracy about it. To go from place to place in a carriage, or in any vehicle, is as literally and precisely and philologically *riding*, as to go over the same ground on a horse.

The discrimination between the two words, — riding and driving, — which a *pseudo*-fashion has attempted to establish, both in England and in the United States, is mere pedantry, without a pretence of philological authority.

A lady says she is "going to drive in the Park," when she is *not* going to do anything of the kind. Her coachman is to drive, and he drives, not *her*, but the *horses*. She is to ride; and she has nothing to do with driving. To be sure, a lady does sometimes drive, by taking the driver's seat, the whip, and "the ribbons" — but that is another matter.

Pray, what is travelling in a railroad car? Is *that* "driving"?

ISSUE.

Newspapers, magazines and reviews are *issued* at stated periods; and, without exception, each of such publications is *numbered* consecutively with the others. The first issued is number one, the second, number two; and so on, for a million, if circumstances permit. Hence, when a particular paper, or magazine, or review is to be designated, the proper term is, "your paper, or magazine, or review of such a date"; or, more generally, "a late *number*, or a recent *number*, of your paper," etc.

But modern precision, or ambition, has "changed all that"; and now, we read of "a late *issue*, or a recent *issue*, of your paper"; or, what is quite as common, and even worse, "one of your late *issues*," or "your *issue* of yesterday."

CASE.

In a recent obituary of a distinguished and much-lamented citizen of New York, a "sensational" writer spoke of the *case*, and in another sentence of the *casket*, in which the remains were deposited.

Did the gentleman know that there is such a word as *coffin?* Or, had he in mind the quaint conceit of Dickens in Bleak House, which is developed through the profound Skimpole? A certain butcher applies for the payment of "his *little* bill"; as if, by using the diminutive adjective, he somehow made the payment easier. Thus, the newspaper writer may have thought that he was slyly administering consolation to the bereaved friends, by intimating that a man in a "casket" is not quite so dead as a man in a coffin.

TO THE MUZZLE.

When a burglar, or any desperate ruffian, is arrested "in the fact" and is searched, he is usually found to be armed with a pistol "loaded *to the muzzle.*" When artillery-men, at sea or on land, grow desperate, they load their guns "*to the muzzle*"

Does any person who uses those overcharged expressions happen to know what would be the effect of loading a cannon, or any fire-arm, " to the muzzle " ?

If he should once *discharge* a weapon loaded in that style, he probably would never again describe the process of such loading.

APPREHEND, ETC.

This is a favourite substitute for *think, fancy, believe, imagine,* etc.

Says a newspaper writer, " Now we *apprehend* that this is a very limited view of the case."

" We *apprehend* that the President misunderstood the Secretary."

Even *predict* is sometimes used to a similar effect : —

" We *predict* that Johnson did not in fact steal the horse."

Of these two, *predict* is a stupid blunder ; and *apprehend* is, to say the least, a *very long word*.

One of the New York morning newspapers recently remarked, that the only way such a political party " could be *resurrected,*" was so and so. And another, not to be behind in the race, said, that it would be good policy " to *placate* our opponents." The latter word is accredited in the last edition of Webster ; and no doubt the former will be so, in the next edition.

A weekly newspaper contains this sentence : " In fact, the opponents of the whole series of amendment, unable to *hostilize* it on its merits, nevertheless object to it as supererogatory and unnecessary." At first sight, " hostilize " seems to be a new candidate for admission into the family; but a reference to the last edition of Webster indicates that it is a superannuated member, labelled " obsolete." Its revival is rather " supererogatory."

The same paper contains this very questionable compliment to an absent friend : " This gentleman has spent several months of active travel and diligent inquiry in the country, penetrating to the Sierra Nevada, and spending some weeks in close observation in Utah, where, through a concurrence of favourable circumstances, he enjoyed *exceptionable* opportunities for acquainting himself with the organization, probity, and inner life of the Mormons."

If that had been published in a daily newspaper, one might suppose that the writer, or compositor, or proof-reader, by reason of haste, mistook " exceptionable " for *exceptional;* for the typographical difference between the two words is not great. But in a weekly paper, the oversight of three men in succession is not so easily explained.

ONE HALF.

In the newspaper advertisements of dividends by money corporations, we constantly read that such or such an institution " has declared a dividend of three and *one* half per cent," etc.

In arithmetical expression, there can be *but one* half, because two halves make *one whole;* as twenty shillings make one pound. Therefore, as in the arithmetical formulas, *two* halves are unknown, *one* half is pretentiously precise, and *a* half is the proper term. Quarters, eighths, etc. exist in larger numbers, and *one* quarter, *one* eighth, or *three* quarters, *five* eighths, etc., are necessary and proper expressions.

NEVER.

Never is often improperly used for *not*, but it means something more than "not." The words may be used interchangeably in certain cases; but "never" means, primarily, *not ever*, not *at any time*, *at no time*, etc.; and, with that definition in view, any one can see that its application to an event that, in the nature of things, could take place but *once*, is of questionable propriety. For example, the birth of a person; or his death; or the creation or destruction of any one thing; as,

"General Washington was *never* born in New York";

"Napoleon *never* died in France";

"That tree, that house, that ship, was *never* destroyed by fire,"—it being understood that each was destroyed in some way,—or, "that house, that ship, was *never* built by contract," etc.

MAKE NO MORE NOISE THAN YOU CAN HELP.

That is wrong, but the correct phrase (cannot help) *seems* wrong; and either is clumsy. "Make no noise that you can avoid or help," is a better phrase, but it is rather formal.

The error of the more familiar phrase is seen when the elliptically omitted words are supplied: " make no more noise than the noise that you cannot help making " ; or, " *than such* as you cannot help making."

A FEW.

The accuracy of *a few* is sometimes questioned, on the assumption that it cannot be correct because *a many* is incorrect ; but both are right.

The indefinite article has a " singular " meaning, but it is also applicable to a *collective* number ; as, *a* hundred. A *great* many, is also correct ; like *so* many, *very* many, being a manner of comparative designation.

" *Many a* gem of purest ray "

is but a later and substituted use for *a many gems*.

Few, without the article, has almost a negative sense, meaning *almost none ;* as,

" *Few* men could be found to do so base an act."

TO PROGRESS.

Much ink has been wasted to prove that *progress*, as a verb, is both an Americanism and a modern vulgarism.

Dean Alford says :

" The verb *to progress* is challenged by one of my friends as a modern (*sic*) Americanism. This is not strictly true. Shakespeare uses it in King John, Act V. Sc. 2,—

' Let me wipe off this honourable dew
That silverly doth *progress* o'er thy cheeks.'

But you will observe that the line requires the word to be pronounced prógress, not progréss, so that this is perhaps hardly a case in point, except as to the word, a verb formed on the noun *progress*." (The last two lines are copied *verbatim et punctuatim*.) To that, the Dean appends this note: —

"I mention, as in courtesy bound, an account of this construction which has been sent me by a correspondent anxious to vindicate Shakespeare from having used a modern vulgarism.* He would understand *doth progress* as *doeth progress*. Surely, he can hardly be in earnest."

The Dean, afterward, and at length, argues and illustrates the question; quoting Milton's use of the word in a different sense, which, again, "is hardly a case in point." But he fails to quote from Cibber's alteration of Richard III., what Gloster says, —

"Alas! she keeps no bed;
She has health enough to *progress* far as Chertsey,
But not, to bear the sight of me," —

which, as an illustration of English usage, is at least as much "in point" as the quotation from Shakespeare.

The conclusion of the Dean is, that, notwithstanding all that has been urged against the verb, it is wanted and should be recognized; *but* he in no respect retracts his position that its accent on

---

* "*Shakespeare's* having used a *modern* vulgarism," is about equal to Jeffrey's remark, in his *Essays*, — "It is well known that the *ancients* have *stolen* most of *our* bright thoughts."

the second syllable is a "*modern* Americanism" and a vulgarism.

The Dean's position, in that regard, seems, then, to be nothing less than this: that whenever an English verb and noun are, respectively, identical in spelling, they are also identical in pronunciation.

Assuming *that* to be the position of the Dean, it is "in order" to remind him of a word *precisely* "in point" — apropos to his remarks on America; and on the American war, now recently terminated. He says — "Queen's English," paragraph 8: — *

"Look, to take one familiar example, at the process of deterioration which our Queen's English has undergone at the hands of the Americans. Look at those phrases which so amuse us in their speech and books; at their reckless exaggeration and contempt for congruity; and then compare the character and history of the nation,† — its blunted sense of moral obligation and duty to man; its open disregard of conventional right where aggrandizement is to be obtained; ‡ and I may now"

* The paragraphs of the book are numbered consecutively, to the end; an arrangement that makes references very convenient.

† This line leads a reader to expect — and an American to *hope* — that *England* is to be made the object of "comparison," or contrast. But the reader finds that the Dean has blundered in his syntax and not in his nationality. He, the reader, is left to "guess" whether the Dean means to "compare the character *and* the history of the nation *with*" something that he has forgotten to put in his paragraph; or, to "compare the character of the nation with the history of the nation."

‡ Might an American venture to ask, How about British rule in India?

[October, 1864] "say, its reckless and *fruitless* (?) maintenance of the most cruel and unprincipled war in the history of the world."

The word precisely "in point," above mentioned, to which it is deemed "in order" to call the Dean's attention, is *rebel*.

Americans pronounce that word *rébel* as a noun, and *rebél* as a verb. Is *rebél*, therefore, a "modern vulgarism"? That is the result of the Dean's argument: *ex. gr.* Shakespeare and Cibber say prógress; Americans say progréss: hence, the latter is a "modern" Americanism and a vulgarism.

Does not the Dean know that Shakespeare, in hundreds of instances, gives a false quantity to words, — nouns, verbs, and adjectives indiscriminately, — for the sake of rhythm?

Macbeth says,

> "I cónjure you, by that which you profess,
> Howe'er you came to know it, answer me."

Hamlet says,

> "What may this mean,
> That thou, dead corse, again, in cómplete steel
> Revisit'st thus the glimpses of the moon," etc.

Also,

> "Tears in his eyes, distraction in 's aspéct,
> A broken voice," etc.

To anticipate a charge, that this course of argument is not quite fair toward the Dean, on the ground that he speaks of "progress" as one of a class of nouns that have, by usage, been changed into verbs, — whereas *rebel* is, on the contrary, an instance of the reversed process, — it is proper to admit, that, in that respect, " rebel " is *not* strictly " a case in point " ; and that the word was cited as appropriate to the Dean's *views of America*, rather than as exactly relevant to his charge of " Americanism."

Therefore, to meet him precisely on his own ground, it is necessary to cite " *one word or more* " that will come within the category of verbs formed from nouns ; which verbs are accented on the second syllable, although the primitive nouns are accented on the first.

Whether or not such words are difficult to find, happens not to be important ; because the Dean himself, on the very page following his aforesaid philological heresy, furnishes three, — *digest, object, project ;* and he assumes the responsibility of vouching for their derivation.*

MONEY. MONIES.

Dean Alford says of the orthography of the singular and plural of *money*, etc. : —

" There seems to be a liability to error in the formation of some plurals. The words *attorney*

---

* It can hardly be necessary to remark, that when the Dean speaks of verbs' being formed from nouns, and of turning nouns into verbs, he must be understood as speaking chronologically and not etymologically ; for, while there is a Latin verb *progredior, progredi, progressus*, meaning to go forward, he can hardly claim that the verb *to progress* has not, in fact, a Latin etymology. He means, no doubt, that the noun, from *progressio*, came into use before the verb did.

and *money* are thus often made into *attornies* and *monies*. This is of course wrong; we might as well turn the singular *key* into a plural *kies*. I am not aware that any one ever wrote *monkies* or *donkies*, for *monkeys* or *donkeys*. And this is not a case of rule against usage; for all our better and more careful writers use the right plurals, viz. *attorneys* and *moneys*."

That is very well, so far as it goes. But if the Dean wished to convey to his readers practical and available information, he should have exhausted the subject.

The rule, which is of universal application, and is not limited — as the Dean's paragraph negatively implies — to *money* and *attorney*, is this: words ending in *y*, with a precedent vowel, are formed into plurals by the addition of *s;* and words ending in *y*, without a vowel, are so formed by the omission of the *y*, and the substitution of *ies*. And a short process of fixing the rule in the memory is, to note that when any word in question *has* a vowel in its final syllable in the singular — as *money, delay, convoy*, etc. — that word requires no substitution of *i* for *y;* but the words which have *no* vowel in the final syllable — as *lady* — do require such substitution.

Thus, *chimney, chimneys; money, moneys; attorney, attorneys; monkey, monkeys; donkey, donkeys;* etc. And for nouns ending in *y*: *mercy, mercies; supply, supplies; pony, ponies;* etc.

But the Dean says he is " not aware that any one

ever wrote *monkies* for *monkeys*, or *donkies* for *donkeys*."

It is positively funny, that, although the Dean failed in his deliberate *attempt* to be severe on his Transatlantic cousins (quoted on pages 91, 92), he here gives them a *really* hard hit, without knowing it.

The Dean is " not aware that any one ever wrote *donkies* for *donkeys*."

> " *Hamlet.* Dost know this water-fly?
> *Horatio.* No, my good lord.
> *Hamlet.* Thy state is the more gracious, for 't is a vice to know him."

Thus, although the Dean professes elsewhere to " know " the United States politically, morally, and philologically, his " state is more gracious " than he thinks, as to the last item. He is not aware of what comes of following Webster's dogmas. Webster did not, indeed, find the *e* of *donkey* " superfluous " ; but he found so many superfluous letters elsewhere, that publishers who adopt his dictionary as their standard of orthography — without, one may presume, having any very enlightened views of their own on the subject — find themselves sometimes following his principles instead of his practice. So that, after catching from his example the bad habit of holding silent letters to be superfluous, they carry *their* practice a little further than the examples go, though not at all further than the principles warrant.

One may imagine the horror of Dickens, when

he saw, if he ever saw, a New York reprint of David Copperfield, at beholding, "Janet, *donkies!*"

Verily, that was a suggestive word for the meddling of an orthographical reformer!

I NEVER MEAN TO.

This is a very common phrase in conversation and in the colloquial parts of novels; but it will not bear scrutiny.

There are three modifications of the use of *never*, each of which has a distinct signification The correct form of the phrase, namely, " I mean never to do so," signifies, " I now intend never to do so." Again, " I never will do so," is a nearly accurate form of the positive assertion for a future course of conduct. And, " I never *meant* to do so " is a correct form of expressing the entire absence of any *past intent* to do so. But, " I never mean to " is entirely inadmissible.

BOURN.

This word is perpetually misused in the way of quotation — or rather, of pretended quotation; for the process is always a *mis*quotation. It is used in this way: —

" Our friend went (or was accompanied, or has gone) to that bourn from which no traveller returns."

The line is intended to be, and seems generally supposed to be, a quotation from Shakespeare — which, however, it certainly is not.

Hamlet, in his soliloquy on suicide, says that " something after death " is

> " The undiscovered country, from whose bourn
> No traveller returns."

And " bourn " means boundary, border, limit, or edge of a country; not the country itself. Independently of which meaning, the construction of the verse shows that Shakespeare did not use the word in the sense of a locality, but as the dividing line between localities. Shakespeare's meaning would be fully expressed by

> " The undiscovered country, from whose *edge*
> No traveller returns."

And, in that case, were the popular phrase to run thus, " Our friend has gone to that *edge* from which no traveller returns," the quotation would be just as correct and just as silly as it is now.

One would suppose that, in legal phrase, the case might " rest " here. But, somehow or other, people are particularly obtuse, when listening to the correction of a widely spread error. They don't see it. They are accustomed to the phraseology in the popular form. They know what the speaker means. The difference is not much, after all. And so forth.

Well, perhaps the difference *is* " not much." But at least, it is the difference between sense and nonsense. Look at Hamlet's words, at greater length : —

> " Who would fardels bear,
> To groan and sweat under a weary life,
> But that the dread of something after death —
> The undiscovered country, from whose bourn

> No traveller returns — puzzles the will,
> And makes us rather bear the ills we have
> Than fly to others that we know not of."

It is obvious, from this, that the locality whence travellers do not return is " something after death," or, metaphorically, " the undiscovered country "; and that " bourn " is not, and was not intended to be, the equivalent of either : yet, in the misquotation referred to, " bourn " is gravely put forward as the full substitute for both.

Therefore, when a man writes, or says — as ten thousand men do write or say — that somebody has gone, or is carried, " to that bourn from which no traveller returns," he caricatures, instead of quoting, Shakespeare.

Akin to this quotation is another, from the Bible, that has gained even more currency than " that bourn "; and clergymen are guilty of the blunder quite as often as laymen. But there is this to be said in its favour, that the misquoting does not make nonsense of the passage.

In Genesis iii. 19 we read, " In the sweat of thy *face* shalt thou eat bread, till thou return unto the ground." But did anybody ever hear, or see, that quoted otherwise than " in the sweat of his *brow* " ?

OPENED UP.

No man can now hear or read an essay on public matters, without being informed that " negotiations have been *opened up* " between certain persons; or, that " this action, on the part of Congress, *opens up* the whole subject "; and so on.

Can any English scholar inform anybody else what is the propriety of "up" in those and in a thousand similar instances? No doubt, "up" is a little word, and it may often be overlooked in a crowd; but it has a very ambitious strut, when thus paraded on stilts.

FROM HENCE.

Any man curious in such matters, may look through thousands of volumes in any department of English literature, without finding *one* free from the incessant recurrence of *from hence, from thence,* and *from whence*.

Yet "hence," by itself, means *from here;* "thence," *from there;* and "whence," *from where.* Therefore, "*from* whence" and its cousins mean, respectively, *from-from* here, *from-from* there, and *from-from* where.

FROM OUT.

Another and a similar blunder is nearly peculiar to the poets. A quotation, or two, will show the way it is used.

SCOTT says,

"The train *from out* the castle drew,
But Marmion stopped to bid adieu."

BYRON says,

"But could the blood before her shed,
Since first Timoleon's brother bled,
Or baffled Persia's despot fled,
Arise *from out* the earth, which drank
The stream of slaughter as it sank," etc.

The recurrence of this phrase is not so incessant as is "from hence," etc., but probably few English or American poets who have had occasion to say what Scott and Byron here *meant* to say, are innocent of the blunder. Yet none of them says what he means.

To "draw *from out* the castle," would inevitably be to *draw into* the castle. If the poets would take the trouble to transpose the two words, — in case they must use just those two words and no others, — the difficulty would be obviated. "*Out from* the castle," "out from the earth," is what they mean: why can they not say so?

ONLY.

Another blunder, of which the instances are innumerable, is the misplacing of the word *only*. Indeed, this is so common, so absolutely universal, one may almost say that "only" cannot be found in its proper place in any book within the whole range of English literature, — to say nothing of newspapers, magazines, and the various departments of spoken language.

A few instances, taken at random from any book, will suffice to show the manner in which the word is used: —

"The light, sandy soil of the hills *only* favours the fern."

"He was elected, but *only* was seen twice in the House."

"I *only* distribute them among the lower ranks."

"They *only* ceased when the day was closing."

In these cases, as in thousands of others that might be cited, the error consists in placing "only" before the verb, instead of after it; the grammatical effect of which is to make *only* apply to the verb, instead of what follows the verb.

The meaning of the writer is that *only the fern* is favoured; that the member "was seen *only twice*"; that the distribution was *only to the lower ranks*; and that "they ceased *only* when (that is, *not until*) the day was closing."

WAS.

The use of the past for the present tense, when the writer or speaker wishes to express an *existing* fact, is a blunder common to every man, woman, and child who uses the English language.

These are familiar instances:—

"The truth *was*, that James struck him first."
"I told him that the Mississippi *ran* southerly."
"Did you tell him you *were* John's brother?"
"They ascertained that the Great Pyramid *stood* on the bank of the Nile."

There is no end to the examples that might be given; but here is one from Mr. Moon, in one of his criticisms on Mr. Marsh, in the *Round Table*:—

"That no doubt *was* what he intended to do, but certainly it *was* not what he did."

In all these, as in all other cases like them, the verb should be in the present tense: the truth *is*, the river *runs*, you *are* a brother, the Pyramid *stands*, etc.

GRADUATED.

This word, when applied to one who receives a degree from a college, is a past participle of the verb *to graduate*, (to mark with degrees, to confer a degree,) and requires some part of the verb *to be* before it: yet it is, oftener than otherwise, used in the past tense of the active verb.

In the memoir of Webster, at the beginning of his dictionary, it is said that " he *graduated* with reputation in 1788." The biographer might as well have said that " he *born* on the 16th of October, 1758."

PLEAD.

In nine cases out of ten, where the verb to plead is used in the past tense, it is spoken and written as if its conjugation were analogous to *read;* and as people say *read* (pronounced *red*), so they say *plead*, pronounced *pled*. But that is not the formation of the verb. It is analogous to *knead, kneaded;* and is *plead, pleaded.*

FIGURE.

Newspaper usage and oral usage have made this word synonymous with *amount*, or *sum*, or *number;* as, " a thousand dollars, or about that *figure*." " The sale of cotton reached a very large *figure*." This is a piece of vulgarism that is just one remove from slang; yet it is working its way *up*, as all corruptions do.

Dean Alford says, paragraph 19, — " has attained a circulation of 1000: no very large *figure*, certainly," etc. *Mem.* Put *that* against some of the Dean's sneers!

MATINÉE, ETC.

Under the present system of education, the French language has become familiar to the people, especially to those persons who are known by a designating phrase that Dean Alford very justly condemns; namely, "the rising generation."

Yet this general introduction of the language among our people has its inconveniences. Many persons use French words and phrases, without understanding them.

Matinée is an extension of the French *matin*, *morning*; and it is the proper term for a morning reception, or a morning musical or theatrical performance. But one of the newspapers recently informed its readers of an "*afternoon* matinée" at one of the theatres.

Au fait, which may be substantially interpreted by the slang term "posted," is a convenient phrase now and then; but when a person happens to use it instead of *passé*, a bygone style, one is apt to think that words and phrases from the French are dangerous to the uninitiated.

De trop, which idiomatically means "too many," or "one too many," — as, a third person intruding on a *tête-à-tête*, or anywhere else where he is not wanted, — is sometimes used as the equivalent of general disagreeableness; which falls quite short of the force of the phrase.

TRY AND.

This is a very common substitute for *try to*, in contemporaneous literature and in conversation.

"Try *and* listen to me for a moment."

"Begin at the beginning and try *and* remember everything."

"Let me try *and* explain away the presumption of such a project."

DECEIVING.

This word is constantly misused in the phrases, "you are deceiving me," "he is deceiving me"; because the speaker means the reverse of what he says. His meaning, paraphrased, is, "you are *trying* to deceive me, but you cannot, or will not, accomplish it"; or, "you are misrepresenting these facts *in order* to deceive me"; and so on.

"Deceiving" means *successful* misrepresentation; and it is not proper for a person thus to apply its action to himself; because his making the remarks, as above cited, shows that the misrepresentation, in his case, is *unsuccessful.* He sees through it.

The verb may be used in a past tense, describing a deceit that has actually been practised; as, "I *was* deceived," "you *have* deceived me," etc., but in a presently passing sense, it is self-contradictory.

The verb may, however, be used in the present tense, when referring to third persons; as, "You are deceiving *him*, or *them*."

The main reason for the misuse of "deceiving" is, probably, the fact that the speaker's meaning is, *lying;* and, in ordinary cases, people prefer to avoid that word for some more moderate expression, which will, however, convey the same sense.

But there is no short single English word that performs the duty of "lying." *Falsifying* is the nearest to being a substitute, but that is both too long and too formal for the emergency.

THE TERMINATION "LOGY."

As a matter of curiosity or speculation, one may remark on the seemingly capricious terminations that are given to the artificers or operators of the several sciences — if they may all be termed sciences — expressed by words ending in *logy*:

Archæology,
Astrology,
Conchology,
Craniology,
Geology,
Mineralogy,
Meteorology,
Ornithology,
Osteology,
Theology,
Philology,
Phrenology,
Physiology, etc.

Of these, one, only, takes *er* as an exclusive termination, namely, *astrologer*. One takes *gian* as its primary and customary termination, — *theologian*. All the others take *ist* in the first instance, as *mineralogist*, etc.; and of them, five others have that termination exclusively, — *mineralogist, conchologist, ornithologist, craniologist*, and *meteorologist:* while, according to Webster, though hardly according to frequent usage, the remainder have these alternative variations: —

Theologian, theologer, theologist;
Geologist, geologian, geologer;
Philologist, philologer;

Osteologist, osteologer;
Phrenologist, phrenologer;
Physiologist, physiologer;
Archæologist, archæologian.

Trench uses *philologer;* and Webster cites Burton for it, but notes it as obsolete. As these variations seem to be a matter of mere caprice, or even chance, without any rule or reason, it is unfortunate that a rule is not generally adopted to make the terminations uniform. This is one of the few cases, where a " reform " could lead to no serious confusion.

WHARF.

The plural of this noun is constantly written *wharves;* but that is incorrect. Wharf is analogous in formation to *dwarf*, and takes *s*, merely, in the plural; *dwarfs, wharfs. Calf* and *half* change the *f* to *v* in the plural, and become *calves* and *halves.* And this also is true of *staff*, the plural of which is *staves;* but this latter word is almost always mispronounced, being made to rhyme with *caves;* the result of which is a confusion between it and the other word *stave*, a part of a barrel, which is *staves* in the plural. The pronunciation of the plural of *staff* must be with the broad *a*, rhyming with *halves.*

The Webster quarto of 1866 has the following comment on *wharf:* —

" The plural of this word is generally written *wharves* in the United States, and *wharfs* in

England, but many recent English writers use *wharves.*"

This is a very easy way of disposing of the matter. It is simply accrediting ignorant usage. The fact, however, remains, that *wharves* is just as much a violation of correct orthography as *dwarves* would be.

The word is one of that class that seldom appears in the works of men of letters: it is rather confined to legislative (State or city) acts, and to newspaper comments and advertisements, and hence its frequent misspelling. Probably it would be difficult to make good the statement of Webster's Dictionary about " many English writers,"— for the word could hardly be found in the quarters indicated by that phrase.

PROMISE.

There is no need of defining a word with which everybody is familiar; but it is very often misused in conversation and in the dialogues of novels. People say, and certain authors write, " I *promise* you, I was very much astonished." " So far from his being able to win, I *promise* you, I think he must lose." The word is used as the equivalent of *assure*, with which it has no connection.

DIRECTLY.

Many English novelists use this word as the equivalent of " as soon as ": thus, " *Directly* he arrived, he called for ale." " I gave him the letter *directly* I saw him."

Hitherto, this use of the word has not gained currency in the United States; and as it has been used in England since the days of *Pelham*, that is, for nearly forty years, we may hope to escape it altogether.

A late English novel has produced a variation of "directly" in this sentence: "*Immediately* the name was uttered, the whole scene of the railway-carriage presented itself to me." The variation is no improvement.

THE FIRST.

"The tyrant custom," as Othello has it, has brought this phrase into very equivocal associations: it has assumed the proportions of something very little better than slang; and it has worked its way up from the lower stratum of ill-educated usage to the pages of respectable writers.

"I have yet to see *the first* instance of a lady's being affronted in the cars." "I have not met with *the first* objection to my plan." And so on.

The phrase stands about midway between the painfully ambitious and the painfully elaborate styles, with a suspicion of the painfully emphatic somewhere about. No good writer would ever coin such a phrase, but he might accept it and pass it without much consideration, — as is often done.

SENTENCES.

As a rule, good writers do not affect long sentences; and, also as a rule, inferior writers do not undertake them. They are not among the prevailing faults of English composition; and, indeed, there is no objection to a long sentence now and then, if it is properly constructed and punctuated. Hence, there seems to be no occasion for any extended comment on that subject. But, as a matter of curiosity, a single instance is here quoted from Trench, in which something is omitted, either in the way of words or of punctuation, that renders both the reading and the comprehension of the passage anything but a holiday task. It is taken from " English Past and Present," — pages 53, 54, Redfield's edition, — and the entire paragraph is given, for the reader's convenience: —

"Looking at this process of the reception of foreign words, and afterwards their assimilation to our own, and the great number of words in which this work has been accomplished, we may trace, I think, as was to be expected, a certain conformity between the genius of our institutions and that of our language. As it is the very character of our institutions to repel none, but rather to afford a shelter and a refuge to all, from whatever quarter they come, and after a while longer or shorter all the strangers and incomers have been incorporated into the English nation, within one or two generations have forgotten that they were ever any other than members of it, retaining no other reminiscence of their foreign extraction than some slight difference of name, and that often disappearing or having disappeared, exactly so has it been with the

English language. None has been less exclusive; none has stood less upon niceties; none has thrown open its arms wider, with a greater confidence, a confidence justified by experience, that it could make truly its own, assimilate and subdue to itself, whatever it thought good to receive into its bosom."

The second sentence is certainly formidable; and the Dean has, in the preceding sentence, so placed the words " I think," as to leave the reader in doubt whether they relate to what immediately precedes, or to what follows them.

BUSINESS.

Why should this word be pronounced *biz-ness?* Usage and all our lexicographers agree in pronouncing

>Lazy, la-zi-ly, la-zi-ness,
>Easy, ea-si-ly, ea-si-ness,
>Weary, wea-ri-ly, wea-ri-ness,
>Hardy, har-di-ly, har-di-ness,

and so on. Why, then, should they not pronounce

>Busy, bus-i-ly, bus-i-ness?

No person can doubt that the original pronunciation of *business* must have been analogous to that of the similarly formed words here cited, and of many more that might be cited; and if that were the fact, its present pronunciation in two syllables is a corruption, and is therefore a proper subject for criticism.

An attempt to introduce a similar change in the pronunciation of other words, as

   Laze-ness,
   Ease-ness,
   Were-ness,
   Hard-ness,

would be laughed at by everybody.

USUAL,

which is now *usually* treated in the same way as "business," namely,

   U-zhal,

has not yet received the sanction of our lexicographers; but, judging from experience, it soon will do so.

In the mean time, would it not be well for the great number of people who persist in saying *u-zhal*, to consider how

   Mu-chal and
   Perpet-chal

would sound as substitutes for

   Mu-tu-al and
   Per-pet-u-al?

HUMBLE.

The pronunciation of this word has been very much discussed, and it remains unsettled. It is a more important point than is the pronunciation of some other words, because the word is in constant use in the Episcopal Church service; which renders a want of uniformity very annoying to church-going people.

Dean Alford is very much in earnest about this word; but, unfortunately, on the wrong side. He says:—

"We still, sometimes even in good society, hear *'ospital, 'erb,* and *'umble,*— all of them very offensive, but the last of them by far the worst when heard from an officiating clergyman. The English Prayer Book has at once settled the pronunciation of this word for us by causing us to give to God our *humble and hearty thanks* in the general thanksgiving. *Umble* and *hearty* few can pronounce without a pain in the throat; and *umble-an-arty* we certainly never were meant to say; *h*umble and *h*earty is the only pronunciation which will suit the alliterative style of the prayer. If it be urged that we have an *humble and contrite heart,* I answer, so have we *the strength of an horse.* The following are even more * decisive: *holy and humble men of heart; thy humble servants,*— not *thine.* It is difficult to believe that this pronunciation can long survive the satire of Dickens in David Copperfield."

Passing by the sneer of the Dean at what he "still sometimes hears in good society," — which sneer, he may be assured, is reciprocated by those who have a right, equal with his, to their own opposite opinion, — his argument may be thus stated:—

---

* Does the Dean hold that *decisive* is **an adjective that admits of** comparison?

I. The English Prayer Book is the end of the law in modern pronunciation.

II. "*Umble* and hearty" gives people a pain in the throat.

III. "We never were meant to say *umble-an-arty.*"

IV. *H*umble and *h*earty is the only pronunciation which will suit the alliterative style of the prayer.

V. *An* humble, etc., is nothing to the purpose, because *an horse* is somewhere in the Bible, or elsewhere.

VI. *Umble* cannot survive the satire of Dickens.

In reply to which, one may venture to say, —

I. The Prayer Book is no authority at all.

II. "*Umble* and hearty" does *not* give people a pain in the throat; and if it did, *'onest and happy* would have the same effect; and then, as the Frenchman said about "the facts," "so much the worse for the throat."

III. The assumption that we must say *'arty* if we say *'umble*, is nonsense.

IV. To say that "humble and hearty" *is* alliterative, is to assume the point in question; and to say that the authors of the Prayer Book *intended* it to *be* alliterative, is another assumption. How does the Dean *know* that they intended any such thing? — especially, when,

V. The fact of their placing *an* before *humble* in another sentence proves their opinion to have been exactly opposite to the Dean's. As to the *an horse* of the Bible, — if the Dean credits it to the Bible, — pshaw!

VI. *Umble* probably *will* survive the satire of Dickens.

Webster's synopsis of orthoëpy shows that *umble* is authorized by Perry, Walker, Knowles, Smart, and Cull; and that Worcester and Cooley respectively accredit *both humble* and *umble*. The authorities, therefore, are strongly against the Dean.

A PLEA FOR THE QUEEN'S ENGLISH.

NUMEROUS references to, and quotations from, this book have been made in the preceding pages; but it requires further and more particular consideration; because it has been extensively circulated in the United States, and has been, to a certain extent, adopted as a text-book. This is fortunate, so far as its author is correct in his views. Many of his precepts are of great value; and they, combined with his illustrations and his generally accurate style, will render substantial service in correcting popular errors, and staying, in some degree, the tide of popular corruption.

But, on the other hand, whatever his book contains of a doubtful or erroneous character, ought to be carefully exposed, so that *its* effects may be prevented; for his faults will find both admirers and imitators.

Before proceeding in the task of such exposure, the author, or compiler, of this (his own) book deems it proper to say: —

First, That Dean Alford first published his " Queen's English " in the consecutive numbers of an English weekly paper, and that he afterward collected them into a volume;

Secondly, That the volume now before the present writer bears a London *and* New York imprint, is dated 1866, and is designated as one of the "tenth thousand" of copies already published; and,

Thirdly, That, although from the Dean's statements, *passim*, in the "Queen's English," it seems that his book has been very frequently criticised in England, not a word of such criticism, except such as the Dean himself quotes, has ever been seen by the present writer; — a statement which must relieve him from the charge of having knowingly gone over the same ground as the English critics; and also from that of having borrowed their strictures.

The object of the "secondly" of the foregoing paragraphs is to show that the Dean can plead neither haste nor inadvertence in his present work, and that he may fairly be held responsible for every error it contains, — if it contains any.

Several of what the present writer claims to be errors have already been designated; but there is one subject to which the Dean has devoted a number of paragraphs; which, if discussed at all, must be treated at some length.

The Dean says, in paragraphs 159, 160: —

"The one rule which is supposed by the ordinary rhetoricians to regulate the arrangement of words in sentences is this: that those parts of a sentence which are most closely connected in their meaning, should be as closely as possible connected in position." And he then quotes Blair's somewhat amplified statement of the same rule.

"Now, doubtless," he continues, "this rule is in the main and for general guidance, a good and useful one; indeed, so plain to all that it surely needs no inculcating. But there are more things in the English language than seem to have been dreamt of in the philosophy of the rhetoricians. If this rule were uniformly applied, it would break down the force and the living interest of style in any English writer, and reduce his matter to a dreary and dull monotony. For it is in exceptions to its application that almost all vigour and character of style consist. Of this, I shall give abundant illustration by and by."

In a subsequent paragraph, referring, however, to the same subject, the Dean quotes from the *Edinburgh Review:*—

"If a man writes in a way which cannot be misunderstood by a reader of common candour, he has done all, as regards clearness, that can be expected of him. To attempt more, is to ask of language more than language can perform: the consequences of attempting it, any one may see who will spend an hour with the statutes at large:—

"— Jack was very respectful to Tom, and always took off his hat when he met him:— Jack was very rude to Tom, and always knocked off his hat when he met him.

"Will any one pretend that either of these sentences is ambiguous in meaning, or unidiomatic in expression? Yet critics of the class now before us are bound to contend that —

"— Jack showed his respect by taking off Tom's hat; or else, that he showed his rudeness by knocking off his own.

"It is useless to multiply examples; no book was ever written that could stand a hostile examination in this spirit; and one that could stand it, would be totally unreadable."

It would certainly seem that this — from a man who has taken the trouble to write a book called "A Plea for the Queen's English," in which book he has with great force contended for purity and accuracy of style — is rather startling. But later in the book, paragraphs 364, 365, wherein he has the newspapers for antagonists, he takes the opposite side of the same question : —

"Just let me, as I pass, notice one defence which has been deliberately set up for English of this kind. It has been said that one who sits in his study writing at leisure, may very well find time to look about him and weigh the structure of his sentences; but the contributors of articles to the daily press are obliged to write always in a hurry, and have no such opportunities of consideration.

"Now this plea either fails in its object of excusing the practice complained of, or it proves too much. If it fails, it does not assign sufficient cause for the phenomenon: if, as I believe, it is not mere haste which causes a man to write such English as this, but deficiency in his power of putting thoughts into words: it proves too much if it really does sufficiently * excuse the writers; for, if such writing is the inevitable result of the hasty publication of these critiques, why is not more time given for their production, and why are not more pains bestowed on them? For surely it is an evil for people to be daily accustomed to read English expressed thus obscurely and ungrammatically; it tends to confuse thought and to deprive language of its proper force, and by this means to degrade us as a nation in the rank of thinkers and speakers."

A proper estimate of the value of these conflicting statements will presently be undertaken, by the simple process of quoting the several examples given by the Dean in illustration of his two positions, accompanied by his explanatory and concurrent remarks. Previously to making those quotations, it is proper to remark that the Dean usually speaks of those who concur with him as "friends," "correspondents," or "critics"; while he frequently designates his censors, or those who, he imagines, might be such, as "*pedants*."

1. "In a Somersetshire paper, I saw that a man had his legs burned by sitting for warmth, and falling asleep, on the top of a lime-kiln. The lime was called *the seething mass* (to *seethe* means to *boil*, and *sod* or *sodden* is its passive participle); and it was said, he would soon have been a *calcined corpse*, which I take it would have been an unheard-of chemical phenomenon."

* Is not "excuse" *sufficient*, without "sufficiently"?

2. "In the same paper I read the following elegant sentence: 'Our prognostications as regards the spirit of the young men here to join the Storgusey rifle-corps proves correct.' The same paper, in commenting on the Hopley case, speaks through a whole leading article of *corporeal* punishment. I may mention that, in this case, the accused person figures throughout, as so often in provincial papers, as a *demon incarnate*, and a *fiend in human shape*."

3. "In the *London Morning Chronicle's* account of Lord Macaulay's funeral occurred the following sentence: 'When placed upon the ropes over the grave, and while being gradually lowered into the earth, the organ again pealed forth.' Here, of course, on any possible grammatical understanding of the words, it was the *organ* which was placed over the grave, and was being lowered into the earth."

4. "After one of Mr. Glaisher's balloon ascents, we read that, 'After partaking of a hearty breakfast, the balloon was brought into the town amidst the cheers and congratulations of the major part of the inhabitants.' They may well have applauded a balloon which had performed so unheard-of * a feat."

5. "In a leading article of the *Times*, not long since, was this beautiful piece of slipshod English: 'The atrocities of the middle passage, which

---

* Not "unheard-of" surely; for if the Dean had not *heard* of it (or read of it, which is the same thing) how could he write about it?

called into action the Wilberforces and Clarksons of the last generation, were not so fully proved, and were certainly not more harrowing in their circumstances, than are the iniquities perpetrated upon the wretched Chinese.'

"Here, you will observe, we are, by the form of the sentence, committed to the combination of *were not so fully proved . . . . than*. This is a fault into which careless writers constantly fall, — the joining together* two clauses with a third, whose construction suits the latter of them, but not the former. . . . . The *Times's* writer might have said, — were not so fully proved as are the iniquities perpetrated upon the wretched Chinese, and were certainly not more harrowing in their circumstances."

The Dean then quotes the contents of two posted-up handbills, and a sentence on the back of a railroad ticket; but no more sentences from the newspapers. That is to say, in legal phrase, so far as the newspapers are concerned, "that is the Dean's case"; and, really, there is not much of it.

Observe the scope of the indictment: —

" — if it is not mere haste which causes a man to write such English as this, ... if such writing is the inevitable result of the hasty publication of these *critiques*,† . . . . English thus expressed . . . . tends to degrade us as a nation," etc.

---

* Will the Dean defend the omission of *of* here, — "the joining together *of* two clauses"?

† In paragraph 380, the Dean, while giving some concluding

6

And the sum total of his *case*, on trial,— for his complaint, here, is not about misused words, but about ill-constructed sentences, — is this : —

Three lines quoted from a Somersetshire paper, three lines from the *Morning Chronicle*, three lines from something not specified, and six lines from the *London Times*.

The errors in those quotations are, respectively, *proves* for *prove;* the omission in the sentence — though the omitted words must have preceded the sentence quoted — of "the coffin was," and the omission of "it was"; the omission of an antecedent to "partaking"; and a sentence in the *Times* so jumbled that nothing but reconstruction can redeem it.

Well; each instance is bad and inexcusable, whether the writers were, severally, in haste or not. But the whole together fails to form that array of specification which the Dean's formality of complaint would lead one to expect. Besides, the sentences cited are, excepting that in the *Times*, mere news items which are necessarily made up for a paper by subordinate persons, who cannot be called "editors," and for whose language the editors cannot properly be held responsible.

On the other hand, the sentences which the Dean proposes to defend against the restriction of

advice to his readers, says: "Be simple, be unaffected," etc., "in your writing. Never use a long word when a short one will do." *Critiques* is not strictly a "long word"; but, for the occasion, it is a very *large* word.

the rule cited and commented on, paragraphs 159, 160, must now be considered.

The Dean prefaces his quoted sentences and comments, with certain remarks on emphasis; which some writers, and all good readers, will be very apt to dispute. His chief point, to which his other remarks are preliminary, is this: —

"Whenever we wish to indicate that a stress is to be laid on a certain word, or clause, in a sentence, we must do it by taking that word, or that clause, out of its natural place which it would hold by the above rule," — that is, the rule of paragraph 159, — "and putting it into some more prominent one."

That is, it is the business of the writer to teach the reader how to read, by violating the rule of grammar, paragraph 159.

When a writer lays down such a principle as that, one may expect, as Iago says, to "see an answerable sequestration."

And now, for the Dean's instances of necessary transposition.

Paragraph "163. Take, as an example, the words *he restored me to mine office:* where the words are arranged in accordance with the ordinary law. But suppose a distinction is to be made between the narrator, who had been restored to office, and another man who had been very differently treated. Of course, we might still observe the rule, and say, *He restored me to mine office, and he hanged him;* but the sentence becomes thus (and it is to this that I request the reader's attention) a very tame one, not expressing the distinction in itself, nor admitting of being so read as to express it sharply and decisively. Now let us violate the rule, and see how the sentence reads, *Me he restored unto mine office, and him he hanged.* Thus wrote our translators of Genesis xli. 13, and they arranged the words rightly. No reader, be his intelligence ever so little, can help reading this sentence as it ought to be read."

Paragraph "164. And let there be no mistake about this being a violation of the rule. The words nearest connected are *restored* and *me*, which it governs; *hanged* and *him*, which it governs.* When I take *me* out of its place next *restored*, and begin the sentence with it, letting the pronoun *he* come between them, I do most distinctly violate the rule, that those words which are most nearly connected in the sense should be also most nearly connected in the arrangement. I have purposely chosen this first instance of the simplest kind, to make the matter clear as we advance into it. Let us take another. St. Peter, Acts ii. 23, says to the Jews, speaking of our Lord, *Him, being delivered by the determinate counsel and foreknowledge of God,*

---

* A person who has any knowledge of grammar will know what the Dean means here. But the Dean says elsewhere that *that* is not sufficient; and that it is the duty of a writer to make his words *convey* his meaning. Now, what does that sentence mean to the apprehension of one not familiar with the rule that an active verb governs an objective case? What is "it"? and what does it "govern"?

ye have taken, and by wicked hands have crucified and slain. Here we have the pronoun *Him* placed first in the sentence, and at a considerable distance from the verbs that govern it. Yet who does not see that the whole force of that which was intended to be conveyed by the sentence is thus gained, and could not otherwise be gained? Arranged according to the common rule, the sentence would have been, *Ye have taken him, being delivered by the determinate counsel and foreknowledge of God, and by wicked hands have crucified and slain him*, and the whole force and point would have been lost."

Paragraph " 165 " recites the nature, use, and importance of a parenthesis, but avers that " every parenthesis is a violation of the supposed universal rule of position."*

Paragraph " 166. Thus, for example, I am narrating a circumstance which, when it happened, excited my astonishment. Undoubtedly, the natural order of constructing the sentence would be to relate what happened first, and my surprise at it afterwards.† *I was looking at a man walking on*

---

* This averment is a mere assumption. The rule is, that "the parts connected in meaning should be connected in position *as closely as possible*. The Dean says elsewhere, when commenting on *too strict* an interpretation of rules, " really, we do not write for idiots "; and the rhetoricians, for whose rule the Dean has such contempt, would probably retort his remark; and add, that " as closely as possible " *means* as closely as possible, and *no closer*. They never intended the rule to hold against exceptions, and a parenthesis is *not* necessarily a violation of the rule.

† Perhaps it would. But the " natural order " is one thing, and the rule is another thing. Hence, the Dean is quite out of the

the bank of the river, when he suddenly turned about, and plunged in, to my great surprise. But who does not see the miserable way in which the last clause drags behind, and loses all its force? We therefore take this clause out of its place, and insert it before that to which it applies, and with which it ought to be constructed; we word the sentence thus: *I was looking at a man walking on the bank of the river, when, to my great surprise, he suddenly turned round and plunged in.* I need not further illustrate so common a transposition."

Paragraph " 169. One of my censors quoted as faulty in this respect the following sentence, which occurred in these notes: I said that certain persons *fall, from their ignorance, into absurd mistakes.* The parenthetical clause here is, *from their ignorance.* My censor would amend it thus: *certain persons, in consequence of their ignorance, fall into absurd mistakes.* Now, this is not what I wanted to say; at least, it is a blundering and roundabout way of explaining it. The purpose is, to bring the fact stated into prominence; and this is done by

record. He is not illustrating the rule of the rhetoricians, — who say nothing about " natural order," — but a rule of his own, enacted for the occasion. And, observe, he assumes the necessity of telling his whole story in one sentence, apparently for the very purpose of violating the rule, though the rule does not touch his case, because the rule does *not* prohibit a parenthetical line. The sentence, as he amends it, is the best possible form; but the amendment is *not* a violation of the rule. The very phraseology of the rule, " as closely as possible," intimates that *immediate* contact, or proximity, is not always " possible," with proper deference to other considerations.

making the verb *fall* immediately follow its subject, *certain persons.*" And so forth, — for, really, the remainder of this paragraph is mere twaddle. The Dean's " censor " was quite right in saying that the sentence, as written, is liable to this misinterpretation : *persons fall from ignorance, into absurd mistakes!*

Paragraph " 170. .... In Deuteronomy vi. 11, Israel is admonished, *When thou shalt have eaten and be full, beware lest thou forget the Lord.* We all know that this means, *when thou shalt have eaten and shalt be full.*"

Paragraph " 171. .... Take another example, Acts xxii. 4: *And I persecuted this way unto the death.* This violates the supposed law of arrangement,* and falls under the charge of ambiguity. .... Take again verse 29: *Then they departed from him which should have examined him.* Now, we all know what this means. .... I must not, however, forget that some of my correspondents find it convenient to depreciate the language and grammar of our authorized version of the Scriptures. I would recommend them to try the experiment of amending that language. .... I have often tried the experiment† and found " that, generally, it was unsuccessful.

This is the end of the Dean's citations on that side of the question; and the reader can judge

---

* The Dean does not say *how* it violates the law.

† " Tried the experiment"! That is, *tried the trial,* "experiment" being a *trial:* say, *made* the experiment.

whether they, with the Dean's assisting explanations and reasoning, *prove* what is said in paragraph 160 (page hereof 117), that if the rule of the rhetoricians " were uniformly applied, it would break down the force, etc., of any English writer, and reduce his matter to a dreary and dull monotony. For it is in exceptions to its application that almost all vigour and character of style consist. *Of this I shall give abundant illustration by and by.*"

Perhaps this concluding promise has been fulfilled. The reader can judge of that, too, having before him all the "illustrations" given by the Dean. There are but seven of them. The present writer is unable to see that the Dean has made out his case — the Dean's case — on his, the Dean's, own showing. But the Dean cannot be left to his own showing; and the question, how far he has the better of the rhetoricians, must be considered.

One's first impression, on reading the quotations and comments, is, that the Dean is disingenuous, and does not write in good faith in support of his views. For example, he elaborately defends the style of the Bible, when nobody assails it but himself; that is, he quotes no criticisms on it, but he officiously applies the rhetoricians' rule to it. That was unnecessary; and his instances are not in point. The translators of our Bible completed their work in the year 1611; and yet the Dean attempts to try the force of a modern rhetorical rule by its applicability to the style of those writers. And then, he requires people to take his word for it, that the language of the translators is above the reach of rules and beyond the power of improvement, — which may be true, and may not be true. The Dean certainly offers no proof of its being true.

But what if it were true? Does the Dean propose the quaint style of the translators as a model for present English composition? Does *he* write in that style? or, would he have others do so?

He makes a great point of the power of the transposed pronoun in Acts ii. 23: "*Him*, being delivered," etc. Does he claim that the force of this transposition is intrinsic, independently of the sacred Antecedent? If he does not, he writes in bad faith. If he does, the same power of transposition must ensue in other cases; as Acts xvi. 3: "*Him* would Paul have to go forth with him"; Romans xiv. 1: "*Him* that is weak in the faith, receive ye"; Philippians ii. 23: "*Him*, therefore, I hope to send presently." Will the Dean claim that in these three instances "the whole force of that which was intended to be conveyed by the sentence is thus gained, and could not otherwise be gained"?

And let the question be here, parenthetically, put to the Dean: —

You say, "which was *intended* to be conveyed by the sentence," — *how do you know* the "intention" of the translators? They wrote according to the style of the age in which they wrote, and the transposition, which the Dean cites so confidently, was not in exception, but in conformity, to the style of the period, and to the translators' own style in other places: as, *see* the three above-cited instances and many more which may be found in the Bible.

Then, as to Genesis xli. 13. Is " Me he restored unto mine office, and him he hanged," so infinitely superior to " He restored me to mine office, and he hanged him," as the Dean avers it to be? He states, magisterially, and as a matter of course which everybody must admit, that the latter is a " very tame " sentence, and neither " expresses the distinction in itself, nor admits of being so read as to express it sharply and decisively." But, " by *what authority* says he those things ".? And observe, his " *saying* those things," and some other things, is what he relies on, for discrediting the rule of the rhetoricians.

The bad faith, or the inconsistency, of the Dean is further shown in his comment on " When thou shalt have eaten *and be full*," etc. ; and on " Then they which should have examined him," etc. He says of each of those sentences, " We all know what this means"; and he offers that remark in reply to criticisms, *not* that have ever been made, but which he says " the captious and childish critic *may* make" (!) on the construction of those passages.

If the Dean seriously means to say that the grammar of " When thou shalt have eaten and be full" is justified by the fact that "we all know what it means," how can he permit himself to denounce the *London Times* for "degrading the British people as a nation" by its complicated sentence on "the middle passage," "Wilberforce," etc.? Does the Dean mean to say, or to insinuate, that "we do *not* know what the *Times* means" in that sentence?

Finally, the Dean really ought to remember his own position, enunciated in paragraph 149 *a:* "I may once for all notice a fallacious way of arguing into which the sciolists who would legislate for our language are continually betrayed. It consists in assuming that, of two modes of expression, *if one be shown to be right, the other must necessarily be wrong.* Whereas, very often the varying expressions are equally legitimate, and each of them full of interest, as bearing traces of the different sources from which our language has sprung."

As to the *rule* of the rhetoricians. It may be good and it may be bad. At least, there is this in its favour : it is founded in common sense ; it has had the approval of the literary world for many years ; and it has not often been assailed. Probably, it will survive the arguments, the ridicule, and the misrepresentations of the worthy Dean of Canterbury.

And now, as to the style of the Dean's book, taken as a whole. He must be held responsible for every error in it ; because, as has been shown, he has had full leisure for its revision. The errors are, nevertheless, numerous ; and the shortest way to exhibit them is in a tabular form : —

Paragraph
4. "into *another* land *than*," should be "into a land *other than*."
16. "we do not follow rule in spelling other words, but custom," should be, "we do not follow *rule, but custom,* in spelling," etc.
18. "The distinction is observed in French, but *never appears* to have been made," etc. Read, "*appears never* to have been made."
61. "*rather* to aspirate more *than* less," should be "to aspirate more *rather than* less."
9. "It would be just *as easy* to give examples," etc. "Just as easy" as *what?*
13. "matters of controversy which have been *still* retained." What is the use of "still"?
13. "I *have been* unwilling to part with *arguments*," etc. Why *have been?* Is he not so, still?
19. "I *had* imagined that their endeavour . . . . *had* entirely failed," etc. Omit the *first* "had."
34. "If we *had* wished to keep," etc. Why *had?*
39. in *note.* "I *had* supposed this form, etc., and *had* ascribed it to," etc. Why *had?*
19. "no very large *figure*": read "no very large *number.*"
21. "A comely thing for those *that* like it": read, "*who* like it."
28. "But if we *do,*" etc. Do *what?* grammatically speaking.
30. "but did not *apply.*" Apply to *what?* grammatically speaking. This phrase is *precisely* parallel in ambiguity to those which the Dean ridicules in paragraph 174: which, *see.*
32. "and *to* them we do not *superadd* another *s,*" etc. See paragraph 380,—"never use a long word when a short one will do."
38. "has been *justified* on the ground," etc. See *note* on page 75 of this book.
39. "*thus much* indulgence *as* to confess," etc. Query?
9. "It is said also *only* to occur three times," etc. Read, "occur *only* three times."
44. "this doubling *only takes place* in a syllable," etc.: read, "*takes place only.*"

142. "which can *only* be decided when those circumstances are known": read, "*can be decided only* when," etc.
166. "I will *only* say that it produces," etc.: read, "I will *say, only*," etc.
170. "It is said that this can *only* be filled in thus": read, "can be *filled in only* thus."
210. "It can *only* be used as expressing determination": read, "can be *used only*," etc.
221. "This .... *only* conveys the sense," etc.: read, "*conveys only*," etc.
233. "I can *only* regard them as Scotticisms": read, "I can *regard them only*," etc.
289. "and also when it is *only* true of them taken together": read, "true of them *only when taken*," etc.
368. "I can *only* deal with the complaint in a general way": read, "*deal with the complaint only*," etc.
86. "*In* so far as they are idiomatic," etc. What is the use of *in* ?
142. "*an* hotel." Authority, that "*an horse*" of the Bible.
367. "*a* hotel." Here, we have it right.
160. "neither of which *are* taken into account," etc. Comment, here, is needless!
354. "This is fiction; but the following *are truth*." Again, comment is needless.
171. "*try* the experiment"; "*tried* the experiment." Read, *make* and *made*.
189. "It *would have been* better if they *had* not *repeated*," etc. This should be, "it would *be* better," etc.
210. "'I fear I won't' *is* an impossible and unmeaning junction of terms. If it *meant* anything," etc. The verb *is* makes the case *present;* therefore say, "if it *means* anything."
211. "he *means* the station-master *to conclude*," etc. That is very clumsy, if not worse. Say, "he *intends* that the station-master *shall* conclude"; or, "he *means* to *make* him conclude," etc.
227. } "unneeded." Query, is that word *needed* in the language? It is not given in Webster's Dictionary.
273. }

162. "at the risk of our *words* not conveying," etc. "*Words*" should be in the possessive case.
189. "As to the *translators having* often judiciously used," etc.: say *translators'*, — that is, the possessive case.
309. The fact of such an *objection* having been made": read, *objection's*.
367. "owing to the fact of a night-*watchman* being employed," etc.: read, *watchman's;* and the same phrase is repeated in the same paragraph.
368. "as much as possible for every *word* being understood," etc.: read, *word's*.
367. "The following sentence, *occurring* in a hotel advertisement," etc. "Occurring?" Query!
345. "It is *most* generally used of that very sect," etc. Why most?
362. "the joining together two clauses with a third," etc.: read, "*of* two clauses," etc.
369. "By and by, a *decided weak* point is detected." The Dean says, in paragraph 273, "Exception is taken to an expression occurring in these notes, *a decided weak point*. But there can be no doubt that my censor is wrong. A *decidedly* weak point, is one thing: a *decided* weak point, is another. .... In the phrase under consideration, had I written a *decidedly* weak point, I should have spoken of a point *decidedly weak:* but, writing as I did, I spoke of *a weak point of whose existence there could be no doubt.*"

Does the Dean mean the "existence" of the *weakness* or the "existence" of the *point?* — for those two concluding lines are *really* "ambiguous." "We *do not* all know what they mean."

If *he* "means" the existence of the *point*, he means nonsense. If he means the existence of the *weakness, his* word "decided" is no better than his censor's, "decidedly," for the purpose of expressing that meaning: and, grammatically, his word is wrong ; and his censor's, right.

The only method by which the Dean could escape his censor is this ; namely, by saying that his phrase means a *point, which, by competent authority, has been decided to be weak.* The "point" then, to wit, the weak point, would be placed among *res adjudicatas*, — it would be a *decided* point, or a point finally decided.

The writer of this volume, after his manuscript of it was finished and handed to his publisher, read, for the first time, Mr. Washington Moon's book called "The Dean's English." He finds that, in some particulars, his own strictures have been anticipated by Mr. Moon ; especially, the " decided weak point"; the pronunciation of *humble;* and the "Americanism" *progress.* It seems that the neuter verb *to progress* is recorded in Bailey's Universal Dictionary, published in 1755,— which *finishes* that argument against Dean Alford.

Mr. Moon's book is a masterpiece ; at least, in its exposure of the blunders of Dean Alford. Its very title "speaks volumes." And any one, after reading it, can see how well deserved is the commendation it has received from the British periodical and newspaper press. That commendation would seem, from Mr. Moon's citations, to have been nearly universal. And, to paraphrase Dean Alford's comment on the probable effect—he being judge — of Dickens's satire on *'umble*, "it is difficult to believe that the *Queen's English* can long survive the satire of the *Dean's English*."

Mr. Moon, however, has himself fallen into grievous errors, while exposing those of his antagonist; and, on the whole, it is safe to say, that, in the matter of mere style, there is but little to choose between the two writers. Each of them is very self-complacent, very "English," and very unconscious of the beam in his own eye.

Mr. Moon has shown great critical acumen in detecting the errors of *The Queen's English*,—pity that he could not have presented them to his readers in what he so confidently assumes that he himself has mastered; namely, "*pure* English."

WEBSTER'S ORTHOGRAPHY.

IF the representatives, or the publishers, of Webster's Dictionary had, collectively or severally, as much power to injure the opponents of the Dictionary, as Webster had to injure the language, the exposure of Webster's orthographical heresies might be a dangerous pastime. For it is a fact within the knowledge of all persons who have read the occasional criticisms on Webster's orthography, and the replies of the Webster party, as both have appeared in the newspapers and elsewhere for the past five-and-twenty years, that the Websterian *replies* have uniformly been bitter in tone, and have been very free in the imputation of personal motives, or interested or improper motives, on the part of opposing critics, — to say nothing of the unparliamentary personalities of such replies.

The writer of these present comments is fully warranted in making them. They are in no respect gratuitous. In his capacity as an occasional contributor to newspapers and magazines, — and anonymously,* as became such contributor, — he

---

* The author of this book desires to avail himself of this first — though late — opportunity of "rising to a question of privilege," as they say in Congress. He hopes that his doing so will not be deemed supererogatory.

In the year 1851, the Hon. James W. Beckman, then a senator

has for many years exposed the fallacies of Webster's " system " (if that can be called a *system* whose all-pervading characteristic is, a total want of system) ; and, as such anonymous writer, he has, on several occasions, been engaged in a direct controversy with the literary and legal representatives of the dictionary. And in such controversies, as well as in the course of replies to his occasional essays apart from regular controversy, he has uniformly been accused of unworthy motives in his criticisms.

The fact that he had, and, in the nature of things, *could* have, no motive other than the interest

in the New York Legislature, was appointed chairman of a Committee on Literature, whose duty was, among other things, to report on the expediency of ordering the introduction of Webster's Dictionary into the district schools of the State.

Mr. Beckman, as chairman, addressed to Irving, Bryant, Bancroft, and many others, letters of inquiry as to the merits of the dictionary ; and, in his report to the Senate, he made quotations from the answers that he received from those gentlemen.

The author of this book was one of the number so addressed ; and. in his answer, he discussed the subject both more fully and more *freely* than he might have done, except in what he supposed was in some respects a private letter.

Mr. Beekman, in the press of legislative business, availed himself of the systematic form of that letter, and quoted it entire ; forgetting that it contained one sentence which should by no means have been made public. The act was one of mere inadvertence on the part of Mr. Beckman ; but the readers of the published Report, who could not know the circumstances (here, now, for the first time related) were likely to consider the writer of the letter responsible for what was entirely improper to be said in print. The thing was unfortunate ; but, having been done, there was no remedy for it.

which every literary man has in resisting the progress of philological corruption, is quite immaterial to the issue. But the fact of such motives' being constantly charged upon him, has always indicated, on the part of his accusers, a consciousness of the weakness of their own cause. If they could have answered their critic's arguments, they would never have troubled themselves about his motives.

The most elaborate of his essays on the subject was published in the *Democratic Review*, a New York monthly magazine, in March, 1856. It was an article of considerable length; yet, it so precisely *hit* the literary public opinion, that it was copied into several of the daily and weekly papers of New York, Boston, and Philadelphia. The editor of the *New York Evening Post* — who certainly stands among the best of American writers, whether of prose or poetry — made the following comments on it: —

"We do not remember to have seen elsewhere such full justice done to Noah Webster's system of orthography, under which the English language has been undergoing a process of corruption for the last quarter of a century, as in an article which we find in the last number of the *Democratic Review*. We have copied it at length in our columns, and we would gladly contribute toward the expense of having it read twice a year in every school-house in the United States, until every trace of Websterian spelling disappears from the land. It is a melancholy proof of the amount of mischief one man of learning can do to society, that Webster's system of orthography is adopted and propagated by the largest publishing house, through the columns of the most widely circulated monthly magazine, and through one of the ablest and most widely circulated newspapers in the United States." *

Such an article, so indorsed, could not be treated with silent contempt; and the people interested in it sent a communication to the *Democratic Review*, which they called an "Answer" to the criticism; but which, in the colloquial phrase, "did n't answer at all." *That* " answer " *was* answered; and, so far as the magazine was concerned, there the discussion ended.

It was the purpose of the present writer to introduce, at the latter part of this book, the first above-mentioned article, with some modifications, as he supposed its strictures are as much needed now as they were ten years ago; but a careful examination of the last edition of Webster's Dictionary, 1866, leads him to infer that several of his suggestions, which were scouted at in the "Answer" in the *Democratic Review*, have subsequently been treated with more consideration. He therefore finds himself under the necessity of modifying his former strictures, in order to adapt them to the dictionary as it now stands.

* The poet and satirist, Holmes, of Boston, says of New York: —

"Where *their own printers* teach them how to spell."

Some preliminary remarks are indispensable to a review of Webster's orthography.

It is an old and veritable saying that, "whoever would bring home with him the wealth of the Indies, must first take out with him the wealth of the Indies"; which, as to lexicographers, may be thus paraphrased: whoever would undertake to reform the orthography of a language (which orthography was acceptable to the masters of the language from the days of Johnson to the day of such reformer), must bring to the task something more than the qualities of a patient, diligent student.

If the usage of good writers, — which convenient term will be used elsewhere, as it is here, with a proviso that it includes not merely the best class of men who write, but the best class of men who speak, the language; men, who, as clergymen, lawyers, or statesmen, develop the power of language by their use of it; and who, by their manner of using it, show the world their capacity to legislate upon it, — if the usage of good writers is the common law of language, language is, reciprocally, in the guardianship of good writers. They are both its judges and its legislators.

A good writer, then, by virtue of his natural gifts and his acquirements, is something more than a mere student; because his intellect has co-operated with his industry to secure the world's notice. He is a good writer because he is able to write what the world recognizes as worth the world's attention. Genius, of some sort, is involved in a general literary success; and no man ever took an acknowledged rank as a good writer, in the proper sense of the term, who was not able to produce something from within which he had not learned, and which he could not learn, from poring over books.

Thus it is, that a man who takes with him to the Indies a cargo adapted to the Indies, may bring home the wealth of the Indies; while the man who goes to the Indies " in ballast " only, will bring back nothing more than he carried. Also, a man who would undertake to reform the accepted orthography of a language, without having first been elevated, by his own acts and by common consent, to the position of a judge and a legislator of that language, will be much more likely to injure than to improve the object of his solicitude.

Besides, a lexicographer is one thing, and a reformer is another thing; and a good writer is a very different thing from either. It so happened that Johnson was an intellectual giant who could grasp the three capacities in his own hand. But Johnson's case was an exception, and therefore his example is a dangerous one to follow.*

---

* Webster's faculty of *word-making* is not relevant to the matter just now in hand, although it is a very serious count in the indictment against his dictionary. His boast, or that of his publishers, was, that a certain edition contained "*twelve thousand words* not to be found in any preceding dictionary." Any one can see that such a result could never have been attained, except by Webster's dragging in recruits from all sources, creditable or discreditable

A lexicographer is one who writes a lexicon; and "lexicon" is, as Webster defines it, "a vocabulary or book containing an alphabetical arrangement of the words in a language, with their definitions."

A reformer, according to the same authority, is "one who effects a reformation or amendment."

A good writer is one whose writing combines grammatical accuracy with a style perspicuous and adapted to his subject; and who so conveys instruction or entertainment as to receive the approval of the intelligent and educated part of the people.

Hence, obviously, the mere lexicographer is the secretary of the good writer. His duty is to record, not to legislate: to say what language is, not what it should be. And so long as he occupies the secretary's desk, his business is to confine himself to the secretary's duties. But to discharge even those duties properly, he must have learning, to know what is correct; and judgment, discreetly to weigh all questionable matters: so that he will follow neither the vagaries nor the negligences of those who may be, generally, good writers.

Hence, also, a reformer is *not* one who undertakes a reform without the qualities requisite to success. Many men volunteer their services in the way of a reform, who prove to be mere innova-

---

as the case might be. And this reminds one of Johnson's remark to Boswell on the proper duties of a lexicographer: "Sir, my business was to explain words, *not to make them.*" *In that respect* Webster would have done well to follow Johnson!

tors. Besides, even the man who is capable of achieving a reformation, must first discover and show that a reformation is needed. His private opinion of such necessity will not suffice. The alleged or fancied evil must be shown to *be* an evil. And, in the case under review, the judges in the premises — to wit, the good writers and their above-mentioned colleagues — must have admitted the evil, before even the capable reformer has a right to commence his work. The burden of proof as to the existence of the evil — showing the necessity for its remedy — is on the reformer. An attempt to reform, where no reform is needed, can produce nothing but mischief. It is applying a remedy where there is no disease. "The whole need not a physician." Or, if the would-be reformer chooses to say that English orthography is *not* "*every whit* whole," the good writer might say, in much more homely but not less appropriate phrase, "it does very well," and "it is better to *let well alone*."

Now, it is saying very little to say, that the only proof ever offered by Webster of existing orthographical evils, or of the need of their reformation, or of his ability to reform them, was — his own opinion on the three propositions.

And, as many persons think that Webster's claims to be ranked among the good writers of English, properly so called, or among men of high intellect and high literary cultivation and accomplishment, are not great; and, as his claims to the privileges and prerogatives of a reformer have yet to be established; he, thus far, stands before the world as a mere lexicographer, whose work *may* be the best in the world, but whose work must rest on its own merits, and not on his pretensions.

The things to be considered, then, are, the *value* of Webster's opinion, and the true character of the work which his opinion led him to produce.

The value of Webster's opinion on the proper manner of spelling words may be estimated by the way Webster spelled words,—so far, at least, as he ran to extremes that are entirely beyond all debatable ground, and from which he was forced to retreat, by public scorn and derision.*

The following words, and many others **not here** specified, come within that category:—

1806.	1828.	1838.
Aker	Aker	Aker.
Cag (keg)	Cag	Cag.
Croud	Crowd	Crowd.
Chimist	Chimist	Chimist.
Determin	Determine	Determine.
Disciplin	Discipline	Discipline.
Fantom	Fantom	Fantom.
Fether	Feather	Feather.
Groop	Group	Group.
Grotesk	Grotesk	Grotesk.

* Observe, here, that Webster published his first dictionary in 1806. He was at that time forty-eight years of age: a period when his opinions on orthography could not have been otherwise than very deliberately formed.

Gillotin	Guillotin	Guillotine.
Hainous	Hainous	Hainous.
Hagard	Hagard	Hagard.
Iland	Island	Island.
Imagin	Imagine	Imagine.
Insted	Instead	Instead.
Leperd	Leopard	Leopard.
Lether	Leather	Leather.
Maiz	Maiz	Maize.
Neger	Neger	Neger.
Porpess	Porpess	Porpess.
Requisit	Requisite	Requisite.
Soe	Sew	Sew.
Sut	Soot	Soot.
Suveran	Suveran	Sovereign.
Steddy	Steady	Steady.
Thred	Thread	Thread.
Thret	Threat	Threat.
Thum	Thumb	Thumb.
Tung	Tung	Tung.
Vaut	Vant	Vant.
Wimmen	Women	Women.
Zeber	Zebra	Zebra, etc., etc.

What can be said of the orthographical wonders of that first column? Do they not, for all time, discredit the mere opinions of their author, in the matter of spelling? Do they not even cast a shade of suspicion over his attempts to speak authoritatively on any department of philology?

A comparison of the three columns — which

carry the "system" of Webster nearly to the date of his death — will show how perseveringly he adhered to his errors. The same spirit, exerted in a better cause, might have been productive of good. But Webster could not be made to understand the folly of his career. His failure to force on the public the adoption of his extreme views, was attributable to their obtuseness, not to his perversity. Scott says: "The miscarriage of an experiment no more converts the political speculator, than the explosion of a retort undeceives an alchemist." And the orthographical speculator stands in the same predicament. Webster clung "to each particular" of his experiments — for they were nothing else than experiments on the public endurance — with the tenacity of a child to a toy, or a miser to a coin. He never abandoned a spelling that he dared to retain.

Fortunately, his successors have taken a wiser course. They have virtually repudiated his entire system of etymology and definitions, and have retracted much of his spelling. The quarto of 1854 is a decided modification of all precedent Websterian orthography, and that of 1866 goes still further in the right direction. Only *three* of the spellings of that first column are to be found in the latter work, — *cag*, (which, being interpreted, means *keg!*) *fantom*, and *porpess:* the last, however, is "put under a bushel" by the brief direction, "*see porpoise.*"

In the same book, Webster's change of *offence* to

offense is retained undisturbed; although *defence* and *pretence* are placed, severally, in the embrace of a bracket with their illegitimate cousins, *defense* and *pretense*. What *offence* " offence " has committed that caused it to be denied the same privilege, is, with truly Websterian inconsistency, left unexplained.

Webster attempted to justify his change of the *c* for the *s* in those three words, — which change, be it observed, was part of his " system " of assumption that great changes were needed, and that he was authorized to make them (he being judge), — on the ground that they were " the only three words " (of a " certain class," which class would be found very *un*certain were one to seek the meaning of the expression) " remaining," that had not been similarly changed by usage. Hence, " it became necessary " (!) for him to change these. He added the further reason, that the derivatives of these words require the *s;* as, *offensive, defensive,* etc.

The compilers of the edition of 1866, in undertaking the defence of the same change, say that it is warranted by etymology, as the Latin roots of the three words have the *s*, as *offensa, defensa,* etc.; and they add that the " *s* is used in *all* their derivatives " : which latter remark is of questionable accuracy, considering that the book which contains it contains the words *pretentious, pretentiously, pretentiousness,* each thus having a *t* instead of an *s* in the third syllable. The compilers, however, say nothing about "the only three remaining words."

The fallacy of the reasons of both Webster and his successors can be shown at once by the citation of the word *sentence*. *Sentence* is derived from the Latin *sententia;* its root therefore has no *c;* and its derivatives are *sententious, sententiously,* etc., which also have no *c*. Now, if the rule of these gentlemen — that etymology controls the spelling of a primitive, and that the primitive controls the spelling of its own derivatives — has any force; it must be of general application, and must *not* be limited to such words as their caprice may select for its subjects.

It will be shown, in subsequent paragraphs, that Webster entirely repudiates the validity of the rule (that primitives control the spelling of their own derivatives) by *reversing* the rule. He makes it "work both ways," — which, in common parlance, is said to be proof of a *good* rule; but which will hardly do, in its serious, practical application to philological principles. But, in the mean time, one may remark, that if the rule justifies the change of *offence* to *offense*, it certainly requires the change of *sentence* to *sentents: there* we have the *t* of the root and of the derivatives and "the pronunciation is not endangered!"

Something more, here, on the rule of Webster, that etymology controls orthography. If Webster appeals to that rule in one case, he must submit to it in other cases. He cannot be permitted to use or reject it intermittently, or spasmodically, at the caprice of the moment. And be it observed — for the following illustration involves that point — that Webster did not limit his changes of orthography to words whose spelling had given rise to objections or difficulties.

Profit is derived " directly," and without change of spelling, from the French *profit;* and Webster gives several roots, including the Latin *profectus:* all of which are spelled with one *f*.

Proffer is derived, in the same way: French, *proférer;* Latin, *proferre;* also with one *f*.

Why, then, did Webster leave those two words as he found them spelled, one with one *f* and the other with two? — *proffer, profit*. Certainly, the pronunciation of *profit* is as much " endangered" by one *f* as *enrol* is with one *l*, — and much more so.

Couple is derived directly from the French *couple,* therefore its orthography is unimpeachable. But *supple* is derived from the French *souple;* and where is Webster's authority, on *his* principles, for leaving it spelled with two *p*'s? Besides, how could he leave *couple* as he found it, considering the " danger of mispronunciation"? Webster should have changed it to *cupple,* — on his alternating *rule*.

In Webster's Dictionary of 1866, the following words are retained in their exclusiveness, that is, they are *not*, severally, united by brackets with orthodox orthography : —

WEBSTER'S ORTHOGRAPHY.

Biasing,   Enroll,
Counselor,   Install,
Counseling,   Enthrall,
Dueling,   Fulfill,
Graveling,   Instill,
Jeweler,   Dullness,
Worshiper,   Skillful,
Worshiping,   Willful.

And, on the other hand, the following words *are* thus alternatively spelled in brackets; a process which at least gives the student his choice between the right and the wrong spelling, although it gives him no direction by which his choice might be guided.

Axe   coupled with Ax.
Comptroller   "   Controller.
Contemporary   "   Cotemporary.
Ambassador   "   Embassador.
Gauntlet   "   Gantlet.
Manœuvre   "   Manœuver.
Mould   "   Mold.
Moult   "   Molt.
Plough   "   Plow.
Staunch   "   Stanch.
Ton   "   Tun.
Bevelling   "   Beveling.
Cancelling   "   Canceling.
Cavilling   "   Caviling.
Drivelling   "   Driveling.
Labelling   "   Labeling.

Libelling	coupled with	Libeling.
Levelling	"	Leveling.
Marshalling	"	Marshaling.
Modelling	"	Modeling.
Panelling	"	Paneling.
Perilling	"	Periling.
Ravelling	"	Raveling.
Rivalling	"	Rivaling.
Revelling	"	Reveling.
Shovelling	"	Shoveling.
Travelling	"	Traveling.
Traveller	"	Traveler.
Calibre	"	Caliber.
Centre	"	Center.
Fibre	"	Fiber.
Accoutre	"	Accouter.
Lustre	"	Luster.
Meagre	"	Meager.
Metre	"	Meter.
Mitre	"	Miter.
Ochre	"	Ocher.
Sabre	"	Saber.
Sceptre	"	Scepter.
Sombre	"	Somber.
Theatre	"	Theater.

This presentation of alternative spelling is great concession on the part of Webster's successors; and it is a favour for which the advocates of correct orthography may as well be thankful. Yet one cannot help looking the gift horse in the mouth; and wondering that men of education could carry so far the delusion that there can be *two correct* ways of spelling any one word.

Besides, on what principle, or by what rule, do they discriminate between the two lists? Why should the words in the first column of the first list,

Biasing,

and the others ending in *ing*, with

Counselor,
Jeweler,
Worshiper,

be refused the alternative double spelling, when it is given to *beveling* and to *sixteen* other words (in the second list) of precisely similar construction?

Again: those gentlemen, in their prefatory essay on orthography, say, as Webster said in his essay, that certain words must be excepted from the Websterian rule of change, because changing them would endanger their pronunciation; how then can they justify their retention of Webster's change of

Bevelling	into	Beveling,
Gravelling	"	Graveling,
Drivelling	"	Driveling,
Labelling	"	Labeling,
Libelling	"	Libeling,
Levelling	"	Leveling,
Modelling	"	Modeling,
Panelling	"	Paneling,

  Ravelling into Raveling,
  Revelling " Reveling,
  Shovelling " Shoveling,
  Travelling " Traveling,
  Traveller " Traveler;

when, beyond all dispute, the words so altered are liable to be pronounced in two syllables? Indeed, if the ordinary rule of pronunciation is followed, they *must all* be pronounced in two syllables, as are *shaveling, starveling,* etc. Who is to reconcile the arbitrary rule that the superfluous *l must* be stricken out — Webster being the judge of the superfluity — with the rule that it must *not* be stricken out, when the striking out endangers the pronunciation? Can anything be more ridiculous than this, — even supposing that the ridiculousness of it were the worst of it?

 Webster's strongest reliance for justification in expunging the second *l* from *travelling*, etc., and that which his successors the most confidently bring forward as altogether conclusive in the matter, is this remark of Walker: —

 "Dr. Lowth justly observes that an error frequently takes place in the words *worshipping, counselling*, etc., which, having the accent on the first syllable, ought to be written *worshiping, counseling*. An ignorance of this rule has led many to write *bigotted* for *bigoted;* and from this spelling has frequently arisen a false pronunciation. But no letter seems to be more frequently doubled improperly than *l*. Why we should write *libelling, revelling, travelling*, and yet *offering, suffering, reasoning*, I am totally at a loss to determine."

The first obvious point of reply to that quotation is the transparent fallacy of its last sentence. Walker overlooks, as Webster and his disciples do, the *requirements of pronunciation;* and that, too, in spite of the fact that the very subject of pronunciation is mentioned in the preceding sentence. What Walker is " totally at a loss to determine," and what Webster and his disciples are innocent of discovering, is the simple fact, that, while Walker's illustrations, *offering, suffering*, and *reasoning*, could *not* be mispronounced with the single consonant, *libeling, leveling*, and *traveling* almost inevitably *would* be so.

But, secondly, — and this, which is equally obvious to every one but the alchemists, is also innocently overlooked, — the very fact of Walker's making his remark is so far from justifying Webster's innovation, that it actually condemns it. *Why did not Walker do what he intimated should be done?* " Ay, there's the rub "! Walker knew, what Webster did not know, that

"The attempt, and not the deed, confounds us."

He knew that the attempt would fail, and produce nothing but confusion, — as it has done! Many men will *recommend* others to undertake what they themselves take very good care not to undertake. Besides, Walker only *suggested;* he did not *recommend.*

Has not the civilized world agreed in thinking that the *name* of our country is a blunder? And that instead of " the United States of America," it should have been called almost anything else? — something that would identify it with its great discoverer, or its, perhaps, greater deliverer? And have not men of mark " recommended " a change? Irving wrote a very elaborate recommendation to that effect, and others have preceded or followed him. And what then? Their reasoning as to what *should have been* is unimpeachable; but reflection shows that what they think *might be*, is impracticable. The essential difference between this illustration and Walker's is, that the attempt to change the name of our country might perhaps have been harmless, if undertaken, though it would certainly have failed: whereas Webster's experiment has not only failed to secure any general adoption, but it has wrought serious mischief, by unsettling an order of things which, if not sufficiently uniform to meet his approbation, at least satisfied the majority of literary men.

Again: Webster and his successors announce the danger of mispronunciation, arising from misspelling — " as *they* count" misspelling — *instal, enthral,* and *enrol*, in the derivatives: that is, they say *instalment, enthralment,* and *enrolment* must be spelled *installment, enthrallment,* and *enrollment,* lest those words should otherwise be mispronounced: they do not say *how* they would be mispronounced, if spelled with one *l*.

The short answer to that averment is a *flat denial:* the words would *not* be mispronounced if not altered. Who ever heard of a mispronunciation of *instalment?*

But the gentlemen do not stop with adding the *l* to the derivatives. They *reverse* the rule of primitives' governing the spelling of derivatives, and coolly ordain that, inasmuch as *instalment, enthralment,* and *enrolment* have been changed to secure their proper pronunciation, — they being judges thereof, and having made the change, — *instal, enthral,* and *enrol* must also take the double *l*, — *install, enthrall,* and *enroll,* — *because the derivatives are so spelled!!*

And yet, after they have taken all that trouble to make their case perfectly absurd, they leave *control* and *controlment* without change, — as if those two words differed in the slightest degree from *enrol* and *enrolment!*

Nor is even that all. *Dull, fill, full,* and *still* are monosyllabic words, spelled with a double terminating consonant; but good usage has for a century or two — more or less — dropped that second *l* in composition, as it was formerly termed; that is, in the derivatives of those words, as, *dulness, fulness, fulfil, instil,* and *distil.* But Webster *did n't approve* of that condition of things. It needed a reform. Accordingly, he decreed,

    Dullness,
    Fullness,
    Fulfill,

Instill,
Distill.

That is, he reversed back again the rule of primitives' governing derivatives. Why he did n't spell fulfil, *fullfill*, is not explained; for, as that is a word in which two primitives are brought together, there is no reason why either should yield an "*ell*" to the other.

The inconsistency of Webster's spelling *counsellor* with one *l*, and *chancellor* with two, has often been commented on; and it has never been replied to but with the sort of reasoning that one might expect from the alchemist, after the explosion of his ninety-ninth retort. The solemn explanation which Webster made, and which his successors reiterate, is, that *chancellor* is derived *directly* from the Latin *cancellarius!*

As to which, in the first place; it has already been shown, and it might be shown a thousand times if the game were worth the candle, that Webster alternately recognizes and repudiates that rule of derivation with perfect indifference.

As to which, in the second place; Webster, in giving the etymologies of the two words, cites, among others, Latin *consiliarius* and French *conseiller* for *counsellor;* and Latin *cancellarius* and French *chancelier* for *chancellor*. After which citations, it is simply absurd for him to allege that one of the words, any more than the other, came *directly* from the Latin; or, that either of them did so.

And as to which, in the third place; if Webster

wished to make people believe that *chancellor* did *not* come "directly from the" *French*, he would have done better to omit *chancelier* from his etymologies: for, verily, the *h* of *that* root places the matter quite beyond the power of Webster's denial of the "direct" French origin. Where did the *h* of chancellor come from, if not from the French root? If *chancellor* came immediately from the Latin *cancellarius* (not through the French), why did he not spell it *cancellor?* On his theory, he might spell one of the words *chounselor;* as well as the other, *chancellor.* And touching the point of "direct derivation from the Latin," it is to be observed that, so far as we know, England *had* no "chancellor" previously to the *Norman* conquest!

After that exhibition, it seems trifling to point out such an inconsistency in Webster as his spelling *amour* with, and *enamor* without, the *u*.

But that brings up the subject of Webster's spelling *honour, favour,* etc., without the *u*.

Webster says that this class of words "come to us from the Latin through the French," *honneur, faveur,* etc., etc. But here, as elsewhere, it is better to admit the *direct* derivation from the French, on the principle that the last indorser is first responsible. He would not have said "from the Latin through the French," if there had been no disputed orthography in the case. The "superfluous letter" was his real object.

But as the usage of good writers had, up to the time of Webster's innovation, recognized the

French etymology by sanctioning the *u* in "the remaining words" from which Webster thought proper to strike it out, Webster would have done better to leave the words as he found them. In his capacity of lexicographer, he had no right to go behind the certificate of the good writers both in England and the United States, as to the French derivation. As an antiquary, he might have gone to the ends of the earth for *roots*, if he saw fit. But all this was done to justify his assumption that the *u* is a superfluous letter. And he holds it to be superfluous by the same style of reasoning, probably, that led him to find the *gh* of *plough* superfluous, namely, that the *gh* is silent.

It would be easy to show that such reasoning proves too much: for if the theory of superfluous letters is admitted as to *plough*, it cannot stop there. It would expunge silent letters from all other words; and that process would *plough* a furrow through the language, that no disciple of Webster is likely to approve.

The fallacy of Webster's position as to *honour*, *favour*, etc., goes beyond even that: for it does just so happen that the proscribed and "superfluous" *u* is *not* a silent letter. The *o* is the silent letter in those words. We say *hon-ur*, not *hon-or*.

Besides, why did Webster limit his hostility, or his partiality,—whichever you please,—to one class of words with the *u?* *Serious*, *curious*, *furious*, *famous*, etc., etc., have also the *u*, and they come to us, as Webster might say, "from the Latin through the French." Why did Webster spare the *u* in them? To be sure, in them, as in *honour*, *u* is not the silent letter. But why not treat the two classes of words alike? Why change *honour*, *favour*, etc., and leave *serious*, *curious*, etc., as they are? Certainly, if the *u* is not silent, the *o* is so: why not spell them *serius*, *curius?*

Again, in such words as *guide*, *guard*, *guilt*, *build*, etc., the *u* actually *is* silent. Why is it spared there?

As to *theatre*, *lustre*, *centre*, *sepulchre*, and so on, Webster transposes the termination into *er*, because, although in every instance the etymology forbids it, — *theatron*, Greek; *theatrum*, Latin; *théâtre*, French; *teatro*, Spanish and Portuguese; *lustrum*, Latin; *lustre*, French; *lustre*, Spanish; *lustro*, Italian; *kentron*, Greek; *centrum*, Latin; *centre*, French; *centro*, Spanish, Portuguese, and Italian; *sepulcrum*, Latin; *sepulcre*, French; *sepulcro*, Spanish and Portuguese, and so on, — because (to repeat, after that long parenthesis, *made* long in order to make the case clear) *cider*, *chamber*, and certain other words have been changed in that way, they having — that is, some of them having — a similar etymology; and Webster's opinion happened to be that the former should correspond to the latter!! Could anything be more monstrous than that, even if that were all? But that is not all.

The words that Webster transposed have — *which the others have not!* — derivatives into which he could not carry his transposition. These are some of them:—

    Theatre requires Theatrical,
    Sepulchre " Sepulchral,
    Lustre " Lustrous,
    Centre " Central,

and so on.

So that, after Webster had transposed the termination of the primitives to conform to *his rule*, he was compelled to transpose it back again to conform to a spelling that he dared not violate; though it would be hard to say *why* he dared not spell *theaterical, sepulcheral, centeral, lusterous,* after he had spelled *theater, sepulcher, center,* and *luster*. By not changing the derivates, he again reaffirmed the position that primitives do *not* control derivatives.

In the so-called "Answer" in the *Democratic Review*, the representative of Websterism hazarded the position that terminations in *er* do not necessarily retain that form in the derivative, because the derivatives of *enter, wonder, monster,* and *disaster* are, by common consent, spelled *entrance, monstrous, wondrous, disastrous*.

At first sight, that seemed to be a good point; and, at any rate, it was adroitly put. But it proves, on examination, to be only a Websterian fallacy. We do certainly spell *entrance*, but we also spell *entered, entering*. As to the other three words, a reference to Richardson shows that they were originally spelled *wonderous, monsterous, disasterous;* afterward, *wond'rous, monst'rous, disast'rous;* and that now they are merely exceptional abbreviations; for, *almost* (if not quite) every other word in the language terminating in *er*, *including wonder*, retains that termination in the derivative; as,

    Wonder, Wondering, etc.
    Flatter, Flattering, etc.
    Offer, Offering, etc.

    Utter, Utterance, etc.
    Temper, Temperance, etc.
    Further, Furtherance, etc.

    Danger, Dangerous, etc.
    Prosper, Prosperous, etc.
    Murder, Murderous, etc.

Any one can see that such instances could be quoted indefinitely; so that the four exceptional words of the "Answer" prove nothing at all.

Webster found *practise*, the verb, spelled with an *s*, and the noun, *practice*, with a *c*, in the last syllable. He thought proper to make the spelling of the verb conform to the spelling of the noun, and wrote it *practice*. His own reason is: "The distinction in spelling between the noun and the verb properly belongs only to words which are accented on the last syllable, as *device* and *devise*, where the verb has the sound of *ize*." The additional reason of one of Webster's accredited representatives — to wit, him of the *Democratic Review*, in " Answer " — is, " The pronunciation being alike in noun and verb, persons are often puzzled to recollect which ought to have the *c* and which the *s*. By abolishing the unnecessary and misleading distinction, Webster established a genuine reform."

At first sight, all that may seem plausible to people who have not had occasion to analyze Websterian arguments. But try an illustration. The verb *prophesy* is spelled with an *s*, and the noun *prophecy* with a *c*, by Webster and by all lexicographers. In that case, the accent does not fall on "the last syllable," as in *practice* and *practise* it does not; and " persons are often puzzled to recollect which ought to have the *c* and which the *s*." Then, why did not " Webster establish *another* genuine reform," by changing *prophesy*, the verb, to *prophecy?*

Again : Webster's reasoning, when pushed one step further, leads to the edifying discovery that, as accent and pronunciation have been duly considered in the spelling of *device* and *devise*, the same rule should be applied to the nouns *excuse* and *abuse*. Clearly, they should be spelled *excuce* and *abuce*.

His reason for changing *mould* and *moult* to *mold* and *molt* is simply puerile : " These words are written without the *u* in analogy with the words *bold, bolt, colt, gold,* etc., from which the *u* has been dropped." Why did not the lexicographer change *court* to *cort*, " in analogy with *port* and *fort*, from which the *u* has *not* been dropped " ? Surely, the latter reason is *as good* as the former. The " analogy " is but a partial escape from the bolder and certainly "original" rule that all words (without regard to derivation or established use) should *be spelled precisely as they are pronounced.*

But it is idle to waste further argument on a "system" that has *no* system; that is not founded *in* reason, nor conducted *with* reason.

The fact remains, that all Webster really accomplished by his alchemy, is a hopeless confusion in the spelling of (derivatives and all) perhaps two hundred words in a dictionary that contains nearly a hundred thousand words. Whereas, before Webster commenced his tinkering, the spelling of those two hundred words, however irregular to his apprehension, was more uniform than probably it ever will be again. He has proved how much easier it is to sow tares than to root them out.

It is lamentable that he should have done a mischief that his successors, even if so disposed, have of themselves little power to undo.

But, on the other hand, it is fortunate that Webster's experiments on orthography, although to a certain extent approved by people of a certain class; have never received the sanction of good writers and educated men, unless in exceptional instances. And after the concessions made in the quarto of 1866, there is some hope that the further progress of the plague may be stayed, as to *all* men.

There might be something invidious in the question, *who does* in fact approve of Webster's orthography? had not the publishers arrayed a list of recommendations in the quarto of 1866, which one may suppose embodies them all. The list is divided between what are sent by letters from individuals, and what are copied from newspapers.

Of individuals there are just *thirty-three* whose names are given; the majority of whom speak in favour of the *great changes* that have been made from all former editions; and *four*, only, of whom refer at all to the orthography: and their reference is so expressed that it seems quite as likely to apply to the *alternative* spelling (in brackets) as to Webster's spelling. The four instances are men entirely unknown as "good writers."

Of newspaper recommendations there are just *thirty*, including one from Constantinople. The *only one* that refers to orthography, expresses his views in these words: "The philosophical analyses, the systematic arrangement of meanings, the fulness and clearness of definitions, the orthoëpy and even the orthography, with many another excellence, — all contribute to secure pure, unreserved praise of this great work."

The work as it now stands, and with the exceptions hereinabove designated, is worthy of the praise bestowed on it; for its entire reconstruction has made it what it should be, — always excepting the uneradicated tares of Webster's sowing. If there were *nothing* — as there is now very little — of Webster left in it, no one could withhold from it the very highest meed of praise.

After so much has been said of *Webster's* Dictionary, it would be both invidious and unjust not to mention *Worcester's* Dictionary.

That great and admirable work is entirely free from the ridiculous attempts at *reform* in orthography which disfigure and debase every edition of Webster from the first to the last, — always excepting Worcester's omission of the *u* in *honour, favour*, etc. But the difference between Worcester and Webster in that regard is, that Worcester did not attempt to legislate on the subject; he merely recorded the words as he found them in general American usage, when he commenced his labours: whereas Webster struck out the letter as a superfluity, he being the judge.

Worcester's etymologies have been always approved; and his definitions are simple and perspicuous in a degree far exceeding any precedent dictionary of the English language.

Any extended notice of a work which has received universal praise would be supererogatory here, even if such notice were appropriate to the purposes of this volume. But it is simple justice to say, that Worcester's is the only American dictionary which deserves to be regarded as a standard of English orthography.

NOTE.

The editor of *The Round Table*, in his paper of December 29th, 1866, makes the following announcement: —

"Considerations of convenience and expediency have led us to arrive at the determination to eschew hereafter the Websterian orthography to which THE ROUND TABLE has given so fair and protracted a trial. We do this not without regret, since there are national as well as other reasons to recommend Dr. Webster's innovations. It is possible that, should these become more generally adopted, we may return to them at a future day; but for the present we conceive that our interest and the wishes of the majority of our readers will be best subserved by resuming the spelling which is most generally accepted. The change has not been hastily made, having been for some time in contemplation, and it has been thought that the beginning of the NEW VOLUME would afford the most favorable opportunity for making it."

This determination, on the part of the editor of *The Round Table*, is interesting to all those who care for correct orthography; and his is not an isolated case. One of the large book-publishing firms in New York, and one of the leading New York daily newspapers, have, severally, taken a similar course; not, indeed, to the same extent; not to the full repudiation of Webster's heresies; but, to a partial repudiation. And, as their course was taken without an announcement either of reasons or intention, no uninitiated person can say just when the thing began, nor how far it is, or is to be, carried. Judging from the pages of the books of the one and of the newspapers of the other, a looker-on may conjecture that the repudiating of Webster, and the accrediting of Worcester, stand, now, about in the proportion of six of one to half a dozen of the other, — a condition of things rather perplexing to compositors and proof-readers. It is to be hoped that, in due time, the publishers and the editor will follow the example of *The Round Table* in full.

CLERICAL ELOCUTION.

A LECTURE

DELIVERED BEFORE THE PROFESSORS AND STUDENTS OF THE DIVINITY SCHOOL OF THE PROTESTANT EPISCOPAL CHURCH, PHILADELPHIA.

CLERICAL ELOCUTION.

It is a matter of common observation, that, while accurate elocution is of the highest importance to a clergyman, there are, nevertheless, very few good readers in the Church. And, although an adequate *remedy* for so widely spread an evil is the thing chiefly to be sought, a brief inquiry as to its *cause* may be not inappropriate at the outset. If everybody asks, as everybody does ask, *why is it* that clergymen generally are such poor readers? anybody may attempt a reply; and a reply must be the result of investigation, and investigation must go back to first principles.

The first lesson of a child in reading sentences aloud in school, is an exercise made up of the simple utterance of printed words, with little or no reference to their meaning. He pronounces mechanically; the easy words at sight, and the hard words by syllabic spelling: the main point being, not that he shall read with propriety, but read at all, — read without stopping. And if it happened to be in the power of teachers to put a scholar through the lessons without requiring him to articulate the words; if the scholar could be made to read to himself, — that is, with his eyes only, — and the teacher could yet know that the boy was **mastering** his task; there might be a reasonable chance that the boy would avoid the contraction of a habit of formal, monotonous, prosy utterance which is universally prevalent among children reading at a school, and which, in after years, is found to be a habit almost impossible to be eradicated.

This first lesson in oral reading is not intended as an elocutionary exercise. It is rather an exercise preliminary to the study of other lessons that are to be learned and repeated; as grammar, geography, and so forth; but, in the mean time, the habit of a vicious elocution has been contracted; and when, subsequently, the scholar is set to reading for elocutionary purposes, the same formality, monotony, and prosiness characterize his utterance.

If this habit were now his sole impediment to reading well, his own increasing intelligence, and the sense of the language he reads acting on that intelligence, might lead him to break away from his habit. But, in the first place, reading aloud before a class, or a school, is certain to embarrass the boy; and, for the time being, few things prevent the action of one's *mind* more effectually than embarrassment. And, in the second place, the selections that fill up those books denominated "Readers," portions of which are given to the scholars for practice, are the finest, the most elaborate, and the most highly wrought passages of our language,—passages which, in an elocutionary sense, are as near the *impossible* as anything human ingenuity could devise, — passages which no one but a thoroughly accomplished elocutionist could master: and, therefore, passages just as entirely beyond the capacity of school-boys — either to read or to comprehend — as if they were written in an unknown tongue. The chance of a boy's *improvement in elocution*, by practising on such passages as those, would be extravagantly estimated at one in a million.

Now, combine the bad habit with the embarrassment and the impossible passages, and we can easily see, that while, in regard to accurate elocution, boys at school learn absolutely nothing, they acquire absolutely something; and that something is error, and only error continually.

When young men, under such a system of tuition, are graduated from the various seminaries of learning, they are certain to take with them *quite enough* of false notions on the subject of elocution. But when one of them enters upon the duties and services of the Church, he is careful to add to his elocutionary defects a preconceived fancy that his own voice, in its natural development, is *not suited* to religious rites and ceremonies; and, influenced by that erroneous conceit, he assumes a tone and manner that effectually extinguish any germs of correct elocution which were born with him, and which may have survived his educational discipline. His *purpose* in assuming this artificial style is honest and commendable. He intends to be solemn and impressive; but he so far overdoes the matter, that, if his performance were judged by critical rules, it would be pronounced ludicrous. In many instances of both young and old clergymen, this elaborated effort at solemnity is carried to such an extent, that nothing but the surroundings of the scene and the well-understood *intentions* of the reader, prevent the general effect from being literally and irresistibly comic. What many clergymen persuade themselves is a solemn tone — or a " holy tone " — is, in fact, a broad burlesque of anything and everything serious.

In addition to this mistaken effort at impressiveness, which vitiates one's entire delivery, occasional phrases are rendered in a way that puts all thought of solemnity at defiance. For example, the words " O Lord." Those two vowels — the long and short *o* — are prolonged to the extent of a musical semibreve: a thing impossible to a man who feels that he is really addressing his Maker; yet, it seems, a thing " very easily possible " to professional men, who, under the pressure of routine, mannerism, and formality, substitute *sound* for *feeling*, and think that they give intensity to the imitated feeling by exaggerating the sound: that is, the more noise they make, the more feeling they exhibit. The line, " Holy, holy, holy Lord God of Sabaoth," is often delivered with this protracted and inflated utterance. The first " holy " is made too long and too loud; and the reader seems to think it necessary to double those faults on the first, and quadruple them on the second repetition.

The habit of prolonging a word with a view of increasing its impressiveness, or in any way attempting to evoke solemnity out of sonorousness, is a blunder in all its details. It is popularly termed "mouthing," and it is separated from true elocution by a distance equal to the entire diameter of the system. It is the antipodes of good reading. If, by virtue of any modern invention, a clergyman of this stamp — and their "name is legion" — could get his elocution *photographed* for the eye and ear, and would examine privately the mixture of strange sounds that he has perpetrated publicly, he would see for himself — what cannot be adequately described.

The assumption that *something* out of one's natural tone and manner is indispensable to a proper rendering of the Church Service is almost universal; yet different individuals hit upon different methods of carrying the assumption into practice. Some men adopt the various intonations of whining; others essay the equally various notes of drawling; and others, again, introduce tones for which it would be difficult to find a descriptive epithet. And all this strange and unnatural machinery is set in motion for the purpose of harmonizing with, and adding impressiveness to, what is serious and solemn; and what, therefore, requires to be treated with simplicity. On any principle of reason, it is difficult to believe that a majority of an entire class of educated men should voluntarily adopt, and resolutely persist in maintaining, what is so totally at variance with well established conclusions.

I have now, at what I suppose to be sufficient length, considered the causes, and some of the effects, of the present condition of elocution in the Church. A matter of much more importance to those who are in the service of the Church, as well as to those who propose to enter it, remains to be discussed: namely, a *remedy* for this wide-spread evil. I approach this part of the subject with diffidence; because, although I may think that, to some extent, I understand it, I am not at all certain of being able to convey my impressions to others. The case may be briefly stated in two propositions: —

First, every man has naturally, within himself, the power of attaining perfection in the art of elocution.

Secondly, he must be, to a very great extent, his own teacher.

That every man *has* the power of attaining a perfect elocution, is shown by the fact that he *practises* perfect elocution every day of his life; and, moreover, he does this not as the result of study or education; but involuntarily, instinctively, and as a matter of literal necessity. Indeed, every child who is old enough to have learned to talk, does the same thing; and he does this, as every older person does it, in his ordinary familiar conversation. Listen to an uneducated boy five years old, speaking his own thoughts, in his own language, to and with his own companions. You will find that he uses proper emphasis and inflection; that he pauses in the right place, without pausing too long; that his intonations will conform to the most rigid elocutionary rules; and, in short, that he will so entirely fulfil all the requisites of elocution, that no severity of criticism can convict him of a fault. And the same remarks apply with equal truth to any person further advanced in life. Any man, speaking his own thoughts familiarly and unreservedly, without consciousness of an audience, and without considering how his words will *sound*, *cannot* err in his elocution. Accuracy of delivery, in such circumstances, is instinctive and inevitable.

If these allegations are true,—and a very little intelligent observation and reflection will prove them to be so,—it follows that every person *has* within himself the power of perfect elocution; and that, if he chooses to set himself about it, he *can* be his own teacher. For all he has to do is *to apply to the words of* OTHERS *the same practical rules by which he regulates the utterance of his* OWN *words*. Therein—in that brief sentence, and so far as the public reading of the Church Service is concerned —lies the whole art of elocution. *Deliver the words of others as you deliver your own*, is the precept; and our matter in hand is, *how to put it in practice*.

The first step in that undertaking is, to ascertain *how* we speak our own words? Well; in the conditions designated,—that is, when we speak familiarly, unreservedly, without embarrassment, without consciousness of an audience, and without considering how the words will sound,—we speak simply, naturally, unaffectedly: we use no mannerism; we do not drawl, nor whine, nor mouth our words; we speak them, as Hamlet says, " trippingly on the tongue "; and, acting in conformity to our inward and untrammelled impulses, we give to each word its intrinsic or relative importance. We, in short, show that we understand the meaning of what we say, and we unfailingly make every auditor understand it; and, by the same token, we convey to him the full force and effect of our language. To be sure, our language may not *be* very forcible or effective; but whatever of force or effect is *in it*, this manner of speaking must bring out; and *that* is the purpose and prerogative of elocution. *That*, also, is the duty of a clergyman in reading the Church Service. He must make the *most* of, he must develop all there is *in*, the language that he utters. And he will certainly do that whenever, by study and practice, he shall have brought himself to deliver that language as if it were literally his own.

To prevent misapprehension, let me remark here, parenthetically, that I am at present treating of the reading of the Bible and Prayer Book, and not of the reading of one's own sermons; and that when I speak of one's " own language," I do not mean one's *written* language. The manner in which a clergyman should deliver his sermon is a matter for subsequent and separate consideration.

Our Liturgy is composed of miscellaneous passages of Scripture, religious precepts and suggestions, general petitions and special prayers. The officiating clergyman speaks or reads these by authority; partly addressing the congregation and partly directing his words to the Throne of Grace *for* the congregation,—himself included. In these several conditions he may be supposed, in spirit, to speak *as* from and of his private impulses; for, although the sentences are known to be printed, and not to be *his*, he, for the time being, represents the original writers. Conventionally, he addresses the Deity and the people in his own person, and it is therefore proper for him to use the printed language as if it were spontaneously emanating from himself. Indeed, his assuming that exact relation to his audience is one of the first requisites of accurate elocution. He *must* virtually make the language his own, in order to deliver it with propriety, and he will never deliver it appropriately until he so appropriates it.

Placing himself, then, in the position of an authorized teacher and theoretically speaking his own words, he must adopt a tone and manner *corresponding* to his position. His tone must be his *conversational* tone, and his manner, (reverential as to the Deity, colloquial as to the congregation,) his *natural* manner, varied, indeed, according to the subject, but still so really his *own* that any listening friend would recognize him to be the speaker by his tone and manner alone.

It is obvious that, in mastering this part of his elocutionary task, a clergyman must be substantially his own teacher. He best knows, or should know, what *are* his natural tone and manner in private colloquial intercourse, and he can best train himself to pronounce the printed words of others in conformity thereto.

To do this, he should begin by putting all thought of a congregation out of his mind. He should, in imagination, reduce his audience to "two or three," and compel himself to speak to the many as he would to the few; and he should prepare for such public exercise by privately studying and practising the language before him, sentence by sentence, until he brings its utterance into exact harmony with his own natural style. This may seem to be a tedious process; it may even seem to be an unnecessary toil; but very few men who neglect it will make much progress in elocution. Besides, the task will not be found so formidable in practice as it may appear in contemplation.

But, on the other hand, I must not so far under*state* the difficulties of self-teaching, as to lead you to under*rate* them. And, in that regard, let me call your attention to one point that may easily be overlooked; namely, that inasmuch as the manner of a speaker, or reader, is the most nearly natural, and therefore the most nearly perfect, when he is *unconscious* of his manner; he may, and will, be somewhat impeded in ascertaining exactly what his natural manner is. The very act of his *observing*, or *looking after*, his own manner, takes away his unconsciousness. A man must therefore, to some extent, separate himself *from* himself, in order to find himself out: a process that, indeed, would not be amiss in other matters, as well as in the study of elocution.

Again, strictly speaking, there can be no exception to the rule that one's natural manner of speaking one's own words is necessarily the perfection of elocution. Yet, there are two exceptions to that natural manner itself, which, practically, become exceptions to the rule.

One of these is a habit which many people acquire, of rapid and indistinct utterance in their ordinary conversation. To them this habit becomes a sort of "second nature"; but that is not the sort of *nature* to which I refer. It is illegitimate, and it must be repudiated.

The other exception is also an illegitimate offshoot from nature; namely, *affectation*. Whether that contemptible quality is born with its victims, or is acquired through injurious training, it comes to the same deplorable result: not one of them seems to be capable of a natural tone or of a graceful action. Everything they do is stiff, clumsy, and artificial. And it is hardly necessary to add, that whoever has acquired the habit of affectation, or of rapid utterance, will make no progress in elocution by speaking the words of others as he speaks his own words. Such a man has as much to unlearn as to learn; and the former process is the more difficult of the two.

Colton thus felicitously describes the difference between ignorance and error: Ignorance is a blank sheet, on which the learner can transcribe what he acquires; but error is a scribbled sheet, the disfiguration of which must be erased before the learner can commence his record.

In the same way, affectation, and rapidity of utterance, must be thoroughly erased before any real progress in elocution can be made.

Let me now interrupt this series of precepts by introducing a practical example. Take the first sentence in the Prayer Book; and, as a universally indispensable preliminary, *analyze* it, in order to ascertain its precise meaning; because the meaning of a passage controls its emphasis, as, reciprocally, the emphasis develops its meaning. The Prophet Habakkuk, in the original passage, announces that the *Lord* is present, and that therefore *all the earth* must keep silence. The clergyman, in the same passage when appropriated to the Service of the Church, *reminds* the *congregation* that the Lord is present and that *they* must keep silence; not literal silence, however, but rather reverence and attention, for the people are to join the clergyman in portions of the Service. If this verse were written, "The *Lord* is here: keep silence,"—which is substantially its meaning,—no one could mistake the proper emphasis in reading it; but it is often improperly read; as, for instance, by the emphasizing of *temple, before*, etc. *Lord* and *silence* are the only words essentially emphatic; but as the sentence, like so many passages of Scripture, is constructed antithetically,— "Lord" and "earth" being contrasted,— the properly emphatic words are "Lord," "earth," and "silence." Some persons contend that "temple" is also emphatic; but as the words are *pronounced* "in the temple," as all who *hear* them are in the temple, and as *they know* that the Lord is *always* in his holy temple when "two or three are gathered together" there; such an emphasis would contradict the spirit of the passage. It could be justified only on the hypothesis that the phrase "holy temple" indicates some place *other* than where the people are assembled. A familiar illustration will make this plain, if, indeed, it is not so already. If Mr. Lincoln were in *this* city, you would say, "The *President* is in Philadelphia"; but if he were in a neighbouring city, you would say, "The President is in *New York*."

You may think that I have enlarged unnecessarily on this simple passage. But you may be assured that it is not easy to *over*-study the language which is to be publicly read or repeated. The great actors Kean and Macready are reported — and I have no doubt that the report is true — to have appropriated no less than *three years* of study to such characters as Lear, Hamlet, Othello, before they would venture to produce them on the stage; although, at the commencement of such study, they must already have been very familiar with those plays. The acquisition of the mere words of the three characters would occupy but a short time, for the individual parts sustained by the actor do not contain more than some six hundred lines each, in the stage version of the plays. So that those distinguished masters of elocution, after making sure of the *language* of the poet, studied its *delivery* at an average rate of less than *a line a day*. And the result was, that they gained the prize for which they contended; namely, enduring fame.

That, by way of illustration. The prize for which you are to contend is not fame, but usefulness; and your text-book is not Shakespeare, but the Bible. The language of the Bible, however, requires quite as careful, and sometimes quite as profound, study as the language of Shakespeare. Every verse of Scripture, and every sentence of the Liturgy, needs to be deliberately considered and analyzed; first, as to the exact meaning, and then, as to the best method of expressing that meaning. And my object in minutely analyzing the first sentence of the Prayer Book, as well as in citing the practice of the actors, is to impress on your minds, by virtue of a single example, the nature of the process which it is necessary for you to apply to every line that you deliver to a congregation. There is no royal road to elocution; and a clergyman can commit no greater error in *regard* to elocution, than to assume that a proper rendering of the Bible and Prayer Book is to be attained by "running his eye" — as the phrase is — over the services of the day on the morning of the day. On the contrary, *everything* must be patiently and faithfully studied. And that is as true for the proficient, as for the tyro, in elocution. For elocution is but an instrument, and language is its written music; and after one has mastered the difficulties of the instrument itself, he must master, severally and independently, the pieces to be performed; and in both cases, the quality of the performance will depend very much on the quantity of midnight oil that he expends.

To treat this point more in detail, the student should practise, line by line, on every part of the Prayer Book and the Lessons, in the same manner as a singer practises on every line and word of a song. He should make sure of the precise meaning of everything he is to read; of the emphasis, pause, and inflection that will certainly convey that meaning to his auditors; and of the tone and style that entirely accord with his colloquial utterances, apart from an audience. According to the subject, he may read somewhat more slowly than the rate of his ordinary conversation; but no other change should be made. And it is to be observed that, in elocution, each man has, and must use, *his own* style and tone. Music is more arbitrary, and therefore less natural. The score of music is absolute; and whoever sings the tune must follow the score; so that a hundred people may sing together, and sing accurately, and sing alike. But a hundred men never talk alike; and if they read or speak naturally, they will not read or speak alike. Thus, every man who would excel in elocution is really forced to use his own style; for, if he attempts to imitate the style of another, however good that style may be in the original, he will certainly "come to grief." Imitation is never natural. It is always exaggeration, and it usually ends in caricature. Besides, what is strictly natural in one man is not necessarily so in another. Men differ as widely in their manner of expressing the same sentiment or emotion, as they differ in features or in handwriting; and yet, in each of the three instances, individuality is perfectly maintained. Let the manner of expressing an emotion differ in separate individuals as it may, the emotion itself is still just as easily recognized, in each several instance, as a man's face or his signature.

Take an illustration, which is extreme in the sense that *anger* has no place in a church: some men are boisterous when they are intensely angry; and others, in the same condition, will speak almost in a whisper; and the latter development is, to a spectator, much the more startling of the two. But no spectator would fail to see that each exhibition was genuine passion, naturally expressed. And were the two men to change their parts, and each attempt to exhibit anger after the manner, and in the style, of the other; each would totally fail to impress the spectator with anything but contempt for the performer's power of imitation,— or, what comes to the same thing, the performer's power of representing true passion. In short, each would then do just what any man, or any clergyman, does when he seeks to express an emotion, or a passion, by any agency other than his own faculties, naturally exercised.

It is, however, to be taken into account that people when under the excitement of passion are not usually conscious of its external display; they do not necessarily know how it appears; but the appearance, so to speak, takes *care* of *itself*, and never *misrepresents* itself. And, therefore, when a man wishes to exhibit an emotion contained in the language of another, his proper study, in the first instance, is, not the external display, but the internal sentiment. He must not work up an expression for his voice, or his face; but must bring his heart and mind into sympathy and unison with his author; leaving his face and voice, for the time being, to their own natural action. The voice must afterward be trained into harmony with the reader's own proper utterance, and in that exercise his ear becomes his tutor. This variety of form, in which the same emotion expresses itself in different persons, is a remarkable physiological fact; and it seems to indicate, even with the force of a natural law, that every man *shall* be, to a great extent, his own teacher in elocution, — as in anything where peculiarity is the rule, and uniformity the exception.

I do not mean to imply that this self-teaching is easy, especially at the outset. If it were easy, and if men found it so, and if men by practice would prove it so; elocution would not be so rarely acquired, and these remarks on it would be uncalled for. But, on the other hand, though the task is not easy, it is also not impossible. Its difficulties, formidable as they may seem when contemplated in the aggregate, soon disappear when grappled in detail.

And, by way of detail, we will now briefly recur to the first sentence of the Prayer Book, — a sentence as simple in its construction, and as readily adapted to a practical test, as any that could be selected. We have already seen its meaning and its appropriate emphasis. Its proper delivery remains to be considered ; and that point resolves itself into the inquiry, — how would you pronounce the words if you were *not* a clergyman, were not officiating in a church, but *were* one of " two or three " met together in a sanctuary, and wished to remind your companions of the familiar fact of the Lord's presence ? For you must observe that the *number* of a clergyman's auditors by no means changes his relations to the individuals who compose that number. He is still one man, whether he addresses two men, or two thousand men ; and each of the two, or the two thousand, is an individual, individually addressed, just as literally as if such individual were the sole auditor. And any style of address — the words being the same — that to the one would be improper or extravagant, must be equally so to the many. Now, in precisely the circumstances above indicated, *how* would you remind your two companions of the familiar fact of the Lord's presence? You of course would *not* utter the words pompously, or sonorously, or in any way *out* of your ordinary colloquial tone. On the contrary, you would speak them quietly, simply, naturally, and *loud enough to be heard* by those whom you addressed. And it is needless for me to add, that your doing so would *cost you no effort*. You would merely have done what you do every day, without a thought as to *how* you do it. Now, would it be a great undertaking to practise on those words, privately, till you can repeat them in *precisely the same* manner, first, to an *imaginary* audience of " two or three," and afterward to a *similar* audience of a thousand? Yet, when you have literally and faithfully done *just that*, so far as that sentence is concerned, you will virtually have acquired the art of elocution; and you will, thereafter, find much less difficulty in applying elocutionary rules and principles to any other passages in the Church Service. You will have mastered the instrument, and you will thereafter have to study only the music.

Observe, however, that the music so to be studied,— that is, the passages to be first analyzed, and then adapted to a natural delivery, are neither few nor small. The Psalter, Lessons, Epistle, and Gospel make together an average aggregate of perhaps three hundred lines for every Sunday morning and evening throughout the year, each of which is a separate study. And to those add the other services of the Prayer Book, which are the same for every Sunday, and which do not require a separate weekly study. But they require a separate weekly *care;* for their constant repetition will otherwise lead the reader into a mechanical, undiscriminating style, which, perhaps, is the worst of all styles; because it indicates that the clergyman takes no personal interest in his precepts and petitions. If you direct your attention to the subject, you will observe that almost every clergyman reads that part of the service worse than any other. Just as a man will write his own name more illegibly — and therefore worse — than he writes anything else. He writes it so often, that he gives little or no heed to his *manner* of writing it. I have known instances of clergymen who had devoted much time and attention to the study of elocution, and who, in other respects, were very good readers; who, nevertheless, uniformly failed in their rendering of those parts of the service which are read every Sunday. And it is to such cases particularly, though not exclusively, that the celebrated and oft-quoted remark of Garrick applies. A clergyman inquired of the actor why the elocution of the stage was so much more impressive than the elocution of the Church? Garrick replied, that, whereas the actor spoke his fiction as if it were truth, the clergyman delivered his truth as if it were fiction. The grievousness of this common fault cannot easily be overstated; for, of all things to be strenuously guarded against and avoided in the performance of the Church Service, whatever partakes of carelessness or irreverence is the most prominent.* Yet those are precisely the qualities suggested, if not developed, by that mechanical style which results from a frequent repetition of the same language.

The mechanical style is, as a moment's reflection will show that it necessarily would be, much more common with clergymen "of a certain age," than with younger members of the profession; because it is a style that grows on all men who do not resolutely resist it.

Many of the older clergymen have travelled in Europe, and have listened with impatience and contempt to the dull, lifeless, monotonous style in which the guides, or showmen, of the public buildings in European capitals describe their objects of curiosity. Did those clergymen ever happen to consider that *their* audiences may listen with the same impatience and contempt to *their* dull, lifeless, monotonous style of reading the Church Service?

The style, in either case, is just one remove from the articulation of an automaton,—supposing an automaton could be made to speak. The only real difference between the two cases is, that the guides *don't*, and the clergymen *should*, "know better."

---

* Garrick once said to a clergyman, "*What books* were those that you used this morning in reading the service?" "Books?" rejoined the clergyman; "why, the Bible and Prayer Book." "Ah," said Garrick; "I observed that you handled them as if they were a leger and day-book."

I am here reminded of a remark made by Macready, the tragedian, when speaking of the constant repetition of his great Shakespearian characters. He said, that, so far from finding the reiteration of the several parts tedious, he always found in each of them some new point of interest that had escaped his previous study; and that, as to his acting, he never commenced one of those familiar characters without resolving to play it, on *that* occasion, better than he ever played it before. That remark — which Macready made to me personally — is well worthy of your attention. It is *very suggestive;* and it covers much ground which you are interested in cultivating.

I do not wish to be understood as intimating, in a recent paragraph, that all parts of the Bible, or Prayer Book, are as easily mastered as the simple quotation from Habakkuk. The Bible comprehends almost every form and style of language, — mandate, precept, invocation, narrative, description, monologue, dialogue, and so on. And the manner of reading them must necessarily be varied according to their several characteristics. But, inasmuch as there is *no* form of language in the Bible or Prayer Book which does not, at some time, come within every man's colloquial experiences, no man can really find himself in *want* of an adequate model with which to compare, and by which to regulate, his public reading of the Church Service. Therefore, whether the passages to be read are simple or complex, quiet or impassioned, they are all within the grasp of a careful, painstaking student. He *can*, if he *will*, bring every one of them under elocutionary control. Some aid may be obtained from the advice and suggestions of teachers or friends, since we cannot see ourselves as others see us; but the chief progress and final success of the student must depend on his own efforts. I have insisted on this cardinal point — a man's ability to teach himself — at much length, because I think it should be both understood and believed. If you lack faith in its importance or its feasibility, you will make little progress in pursuing it.

If any of you would take the trouble to watch the familiar conversation of two or more persons, young or old, you would discover one fact, which, unless your attention has been previously directed to the subject, you may have never yet known or thought of, — namely, that the tones of the several speakers run through almost every note of a musical octave, and that hardly three consecutive words are uttered in, or on, the same note. That is to say, ordinary and natural conversation is unconsciously carried on in a *great variety* of tones. Yet, let one of those talkers, in the midst of that conversation, *read* a paragraph from a book or a newspaper, and he will immediately assume a monotonous utterance, rendering entire lines on a single note, and probably giving the last word of every sentence also on one, but a lower, note. He will almost certainly do this — that is, end all his sentences on one note — if he reads the Bible. For of all methods that human ingenuity could devise, if employed for the express purpose of rendering good reading impossible, the division of the Bible into verses is the best.

We are so accustomed to this typographical arrangement, that we are not only resigned to it, but we are also partly insensible to its great defects. Yet a moment's consideration as to the effect of a similar disfiguration of any other book — the "Spectator," for example — would show its inherent monstrosity. The single and imaginary advantage of this division is, its facilitating the search for any particular passage; but for all ordinary occasions — indeed for any occasion — the designation of a *chapter* is sufficiently explicit: while the *dis*advantages of the division are *real*, and of paramount importance. Such a division is, in fact, equivalent to printing the Bible in a new language; or, at least, a language newly constructed and subject to new laws of composition: a language, or a style of language, that is perverted from the form in which its original translators presented it to the world, and that is an abrogation of the form in which any living language is printed.

One essential principle of printed or written language is, the assignment of a separate section or paragraph to each division, or branch, of a subject, — an arrangement originating in a literal necessity, — an arrangement that simplifies the comprehension of what is written to a degree that, perhaps,

is fully appreciated only when it is repudiated.
The eye and the mind of a reader rest on, and depend on, the paragraphical divisions as on beacons
or landmarks; and when those are in sight, he
proceeds safely and confidently on his voyage; but
when they are removed, — or, what is worse, when
they are replaced by false beacons, — he cannot be
sure of his course. He may have studied his way
by the chart, and may think that he has mastered
its sinuosities; but the misleading power of the
verse divisions — which *seem* to be guides and are
not — constantly betrays him into difficulty. And,
as if this minute and perplexing subdivision were
not enough, many editions of the Bible are cumbered with asterisks, letters, and numbers, referring to marginal notes, and with interpolated parallel readings; and all these are so intermingled
with the punctuation, that, to renew the metaphor,
the channel is choked with shallows and snags, and
no amount of coolness, skill, or foresight can carry
the navigator safely through its perils. The act of
reading through clearly defined paragraphs is quite
enough to tax all the powers of a reader; it is all
he can do to read well, when his course is free from
typographical obstacles; and his mind and eye are
sufficiently occupied while rendering language that
is divested of adventitious impediments: but when
his attention is divided between the ship and the
rocks, — when he must keep one eye on the engine
and another on the wheel, — his faculties become
overtasked, and he can hardly escape shipwreck.

In these circumstances, a due regard to the various requisites of elocution is impossible; but the reader of the Bible in verses is apt not only to read ill generally; he is also apt to read ill particularly, in the matter of a constantly recurring period on one note. It is common, in the reading of any other book, for the reader to begin a *paragraph* on one note, and end it, also, on one note; but the usual *length* of a paragraph prevents the sound of *that* from becoming disagreeable, or observable. It is harmless from its infrequency. But when the same thing occurs at the end of every second or third *line*, it becomes offensive by its dull, unmeaning monotony. It degenerates from *reading* to a sort of *recitative;* the words fall successively on the ear without reaching the understanding, as drops of water from a leaky reservoir, in ever-beginning, never-ending routine; and the effect on an auditor's nerves is the same as would be produced by *any* succession of sounds that have no meaning whatever: — as, one, two, three, four, *five`;* one, two, three, *four`;* one, two, three, four, five, six, seven, eight, *nine`;* one, two, *three`;* and so on, the single characteristic being the utterance of every word *but* the last on one note, and the last also always on one, but a lower, note. This may seem to be exaggerated. But if you will listen to any ordinary reading of the Bible, keeping this point in mind, you will not listen *often* without hearing precisely that succession of dull, uniform sounds.

One remedy for *this* obstacle to good reading is,

the use of a Paragraph Bible, of which two or three editions are extant. I wish they were more common; and I doubt whether the American Bible Society could render to elocution a service greater than *making* them so.

One thing more remains to be said on this subject, — namely, a suggestion on the *injury to the voice*, produced by the habit of monotonous delivery.

You are all aware, from your own observation, that a man can *talk* through a whole evening with less fatigue to his vocal organs than would ensue from his *reading* half an hour. *Why is this?* The human voice is like a stringed instrument of music. It has a certain number — more or less in individual cases — of tones, or notes; and, in common conversation, almost every one of these notes is brought into use: and, when used properly, each is kept in order, and even *improved*, by use. But if two or three only are used, as in monotonous reading, they become fatigued and permanently injured by being used too much; while the others become rusty, weak, discordant, from not being used at all. In other words, and to drop the metaphor, the diseases of the throat, so common among the clergy, are easily and directly traced to their habit of monotonous delivery.

The next point to which I would call your attention is *audibleness;* a matter, in one respect, more important than any other principle of elocution; for, if a clergyman's words cannot be *heard* by his congregation, it is quite immaterial how well or ill they are delivered.

The want of audibleness prevails to a greater extent among clergymen than, probably, they themselves are aware. Many of them, even, who have great vocal power, and are conscious that the sound of their voices fills a church, are still entirely deficient in distinct articulation, because they project the words from the roof of the mouth instead of from their lips; and the result is a confusion of sounds without any syllabication. Others speak from the throat in a hollow, sepulchral tone, and with an elaboration of syllables and emphasis so mixed together that no ear can eliminate the individual words. Others, again, drop the voice to a whisper at the end of a sentence; and, as this habit, like any habit good or bad, increases by use, they eventually pronounce not only the last word, but many preceding words, in the same low tone. Others have a trick of *clipping* their words, which sacrifices a considerable proportion of monosyllables, and reduces words of three or four syllables, to two. And, again, some men of a sensitive temperament allow their feelings to run away with their faculties in impassioned or pathetic sentences, so that their utterance is impeded or choked by the internal impulse, and distinct articulation becomes impossible.

Those five specifications include readers or speakers who are unconscious of being inaudible, and who, therefore, are at no pains to amend their errors. But there is a large class of clergymen who know the difficulty of making themselves heard, without knowing the right method to overcome it. Their custom is to raise the voice a note or two above its natural key, and then exert all their vocal power upon that false key. This soon exhausts the speaker, but it does not help the hearer. Every man has one natural key, and the moment he abandons that, he loses all proper control of his voice; he has little power over his emphasis, and none over his modulations or inflections; and his utterances, like false coin, come back to him without having performed their office.

And in addition to these specified causes of inaudibleness, there remains the entire category of elocutionary faults that I have already designated as appertaining to any delivery that is artificial, — anything out of one's own tone and manner. In short, each and every form of vocal utterance which is not literally and strictly the *natural* manner of the speaker or reader, apart from an audience, will certainly be inaudible in the exact ratio of its variation from nature. So that the various styles of false elocution not only fail to catch the sympathy of an auditor, but they also, in proportion as they are false, fail to reach his ears.

On the other hand, the correct elocutionist succeeds in every point where the pretenders fail. For, when he has once brought his tone and manner to the requisite standard, he has but to throw additional force into his voice, *without raising its key*, and he will be distinctly heard in any part of a church that is properly constructed and is of moderate size. This principle is perfectly simple, and it is corroborated by the same principle in music. A church choir, if practising in a parlour, will necessarily preserve the *key* of the several tunes, while, however, they graduate the force of their voices to the size of the apartment; and when they practise or sing in a church, they give their full power of voice, but still always on the same key. If they should change the key, they would not be heard the better, but their rendering of the music would be altogether the worse, by *reason* of the change.

I have now submitted to your consideration the subjects, severally, of natural and affected delivery; audible and inaudible delivery; and the importance of a careful study of what is to be delivered, in the various services of the Church. And, thus far, I have entered but slightly upon practical illustration, because to do so would require more time than is now at my disposal. But I must warn you against disregarding the precepts you have heard, on the ground that they have not been more fully supported by illustrations. No man can safely flatter himself that the obstacles to good reading are imaginary, or that *he* has a peculiar faculty for overcoming them without labour. Such an opinion would prove nothing but his own obtuseness, and it would certainly be *reversed* by his auditors. He may deceive himself, but he cannot deceive them. True elocution goes straight to the understanding and the heart; every listener is a judge of it by in stinct; and bad reading must create dissatisfaction, though it may not elicit open complaint.

And it is by no means as a mere matter of taste, or in subordination to exacting criticism, that accurate elocution is to be required at the hands of the clergy. Men must be taken as they are. They must be dealt with, by their spiritual teacher, according to their infirmities. They may be unreasonable in their tacit, or expressed, demands for the outward accomplishments of a clergyman. But the one great duty of those who preach the Gospel is to call sinners to repentance; and they should labour to make that call effectual by adapting it to human weaknesses, and by embellishing it with all the attractions which their ability can supply. The greater the apathy or the obstinacy of the hearer, the more need is there for the impressive and persuasive elocution of the preacher. And, surely, no amount of time, care, or study devoted to *that* end, can be said to be *lost*.

When you come to apply these general principles to the delivery of particular parts of the service, and when you have thoroughly ascertained the meaning of what is before you, *emphasis* becomes your primary consideration. By way of an example, we will take a sentence in which — excepting, indeed, audibleness — emphasis is the sole elocutionary requisite; for it is so simply constructed that neither pause nor inflection has much to do with its proper delivery; and, if the emphasis is rightly placed, the meaning cannot be mistaken;

while, on the other hand, a wrong emphasis completely neutralizes the spirit of the words. I refer to the ninth commandment.

Strange as it is, it is not the less true, that this passage is read wrong more commonly than, perhaps, any other in the Bible. One reason for this is, probably, that each of the four commandments, from the sixth to the ninth, contains a single prohibitory precept in a single line; and, in the first three, the substance of the prohibition lies in the last word; so that when the reader, by a sort of routine, has said, "Thou shalt do no *murder*"; "Thou shalt not commit *adultery*"; "Thou shalt not *steal*"; it would seem to be, as it generally proves to be, a matter of course that he should add, "Thou shalt not bear false-witness against thy *neighbour*." But "neighbour" is no part of the *gravamen* of the prohibition. If it were so, false-witness against any one else would not be interdicted by the mandate. The essence of the interdict is *false-witness;* as is shown, if proof were needed, by our Saviour's recapitulation of the commandments to the young man who "had great possessions," Matthew xix. Some clergymen, with similar want of reflection, place the emphasis on "against"; thus virtually implying that false-witness in a neighbour's *favour* might be permitted. But the true reading renders literally *un*emphatic every word except the thing forbidden; and as the last three words are, in an elocutionary sense, superfluous, they should, as to emphasis, be disregarded; thus, "Thou shalt not bear *false-witness* against thy neighbour."

And here let me remark, briefly, that a slight pause after — or, according to the form of the sentence, before — an emphatic word, adds force to the emphasis. A very little addition to the voice, followed — or, in certain cases, preceded — by a momentary pause, gives, in fact, a better effect than speaking a word in a loud tone.

There is another class of instances where a wrong emphasis is very common, without being fatal to the sense of the passage, although the error weakens its force. For example, the phrases "King *of* kings," "Lord *of* lords," "Hebrew *of* the Hebrews," etc. The preposition is here used *out* of its ordinary sense, and it signifies *over, above, chief among;* and that meaning comes out distinctly with the emphasis, making the difference between "Lord of *lords*" and "Lord *of* lords" obvious to the most superficial observation. And if an "of" is thus important, an *and* may be even more so. "Ye cannot serve God and *Mammon*," is the usual reading of that line; yet that reading implies something in *common* between the two names; whereas, "God *and* Mammon" develops the antithesis, which is the point of the assertion.

Those are a few of the simple passages that are almost constantly *mis*read; which shows how little care clergymen bestow on *what* they read; and it therefore is not strange that the niceties of more complex sentences are overlooked. Examples of the latter kind are abundant; but as I am just now citing the force of small words, we will take the " it " of the fourth verse of the twelfth chapter of the Second Book of Samuel: " And there came a *traveller* unto the *rich* man, and *he spared* to take of his *own* flock, and of his *own* herd, to *dress* for the wayfaring man that was come unto him; but took the *poor* man's *lamb* and dressed *it* for the man that was come to him."

In the twenty-sixth verse of the ninth chapter of St. John, there is an instance of the power of emphatic monosyllables, *when accompanied by the rising inflection.* And as this is my first particular reference to inflections, I will mention the rule that regulates them when applied to interrogatories. The rule is, that questions which need a response of *yes* or *no*, require the rising, and all other questions, the falling, inflection. The rule is general; but, as applied to isolated inquiries, it is a rule almost without an exception. In the verse referred to, you will see that the emphasizing of " what " and " how," with a *disregard* of the rule of inflection, suggests, even to one who has not heard the preceding verses of the chapter, that the two questions are a *repetition*, in brief, of what has already been asked at more length. And not only so, but — what is much more relative to the principle I have insisted on, namely, the importance of making the language of others our own — that emphasis and that inflection are certainly just what the actual speakers in the Gospel narrative would have used. The verse referred to is, " Then said they to him again, *What* did he to thee? *how* opened he thine eyes?"

I will give one more example of the importance of mere emphasis, apart from other elements of elocution; and this is worthy of notice from the fact, that, while the passage in Matthew requires a certain emphasis to develop its full force, the same words in Luke require a different emphasis, by reason of the occurrence of the word " prophet " in the immediately preceding verse. The verses are, respectively, the thirty-seventh of the twenty-third chapter of Matthew, and the thirty-third and thirty-fourth of the thirteenth chapter of Luke. In Matthew we read: " O Jerusalem, Jerusalem, thou that killest the *prophets*, and stonest them which are *sent* unto thee, how often would *I* have gathered thy children together, even as a hen gathereth her chickens under her wings, and *ye* would *not!*"

It can hardly be necessary to call your attention to the additional force given to that verse by changing the emphasis from " killest " and " stonest," which is the common reading, to *prophets* and *sent;* the change makes obvious the difference in aggravation between the two crimes of, so to speak, a common murder and the murder of one sent from God. But that emphasis cannot be properly given to the same words in Luke, because the preceding verse is: " Nevertheless, I must *walk* to-day and to-morrow, *and* the day following: for it *cannot* be that a *prophet* perish *out* of Jerusalem." As "prophet" is used in this verse, and is emphatic, it cannot properly be emphasized again in the very next line.

The second sentence of the Prayer Book, "From the rising," etc., is another instance of a passage that requires a change of reading with a change of connection: the change of reading, however, is not one of emphasis, but of inflection, and it develops the comparative power of the rising and falling inflection in the particular case. The verse is the eleventh of the first chapter of Malachi, and it is adopted into the Prayer Book with the omission of its first word; which word is essential in the context by reason of its connection; but is superfluous in the Liturgy, because the prophecy is there used independently of antecedents.

Malachi, in the tenth verse, denounces the irreligion of the Israelites; and, in the eleventh, contrasts their condition with the coming state of the Gentiles. The eleventh verse commences with the word "For," which is omitted in the Prayer Book. "*For*" is here equivalent to *but*, as will soon be shown; but the whole verse, as quoted in the Prayer Book, should first be analyzed.

The antithesis of the rising and setting sun unmistakably indicates the proper emphasis of that phrase; but the reference to the sun's apparent motion is one of *locality*, not of *time;* it does not mean from the *hour* of the rising to the setting, but from the *place* of the rising to the setting,—that is, over the whole earth. And hence, in the second clause of the verse, "every place" is not emphatic, because that phrase is virtually a *repetition* as to *space occupied*, or to be occupied, while it contains an additional prophecy relative to the *works*, as the first clause of the verse relates to the *faith*, of the Gentiles. Therefore, the "*incense*" offered becomes emphatic in that clause, as does the *quality* of the offering — "*pure*" — in the second clause. And in the third clause — which is a repetition as to the "*Name*" of the Lord, but which refers to a people other than Jew or Gentile, namely, the heathen — that term becomes emphatic. The reading of the Prayer Book version is, therefore, "From the *rising* of the sun, even unto the going *down* of the same, my name shall be *great* among the *Gentiles*; and in every place *incense* shall be offered unto my name, and a *pure* offering: for my name shall be great among the *heathen*, saith the Lord of hosts."

But when the tenth and eleventh verses of Malachi are taken together, a different reading becomes necessary. Thus: "Who is there even among *you* that would shut the doors for *nought?* neither do ye kindle fire on mine *altar* for nought. I have no pleasure *in* you, saith the Lord of hosts, neither will I accept an offering at your *hand*." "For," [that is, *but*] "from the *rising* of the sun even unto the going *down* of the same, my name shall be great among the *Gentiles*," etc.

Now apply the *falling* inflection to the "Gentiles," and you will see the difference: "I have no pleasure *in* you, neither will I accept an offering **at** your *hand*. But from the *rising* of the sun even unto the going *down* of the same, my name shall be great among the *Gentiles*."

You perceive how much force is given to the passage by the rising inflection on "Gentiles," though you may not perceive the reason. And, for my own part, I must confess that I am not prepared to enlighten you. The difference between the two inflections strikes my ear and commends itself to my judgment by a process much shorter than reasoning, and I feel the result without being able to account for it.

In one respect this citation is of no practical importance, because the first chapter of Malachi is not appointed to be read in the Church Service; but it furnishes another example of the proper method of analyzing a sentence for the purpose of ascertaining its emphatic words; and it is another proof of the power of the rising inflection, in certain cases.

Perhaps no instance of the power of a false emphasis to destroy the meaning of a passage, is more striking than one that can be applied to the eighteenth verse of the second chapter of St. Matthew:

"In Rama was there a voice heard; lamentation, and weeping, and great mourning; Rachel weeping for her children, and would not be comforted, because they *are* not": that is, because they *live* not, exist not: which is one of the meanings of the verb *to be*, though it is seldom so used at present. "Are" is, of course, the emphatic word in the last line. But see the result of transferring the emphasis to *they!* —

"Rachel weeping for her children, and would not be comforted, because *they* are not": which has the strange effect of rendering a repetition of "comforted," an *understood* part of the sentence, and which changes the meaning to, "Rachel would not be comforted because her children are not comforted."

These few instances serve to show the great importance of emphasis, and the necessity for a careful study of even the most simple sentence, in order to ascertain its emphatic words. But we must remember, that, while a *neglect* of emphasis is fatal to elocution, the *abuse* of it is equally disastrous. To overdo it is as bad as to omit it. Indeed, the two things come to the same result; for, if emphasis is distributed indiscriminately, it, like indiscriminately lavished honours, ceases to have any value whatever. If a sentence has but two emphatic words, and, nevertheless, thrice that number are emphasized; all the distinction aimed at, is lost. I enlarge on this truism, because many readers fall into this error. In their anxiety to make the most of a sentence, they emphasize it down to zero. It follows, then, that, as there is no manual, or formulary, by which emphatic words may be ascertained, their discovery must be left to study and to "private judgment." As Hamlet says, "your *own discretion* must be your tutor." And thus, ir regard to this branch of our subject, we come back to the cardinal point, so often insisted on, — that a man at least *may* be his own teacher. For, any man of cultivation and ordinary intelligence *can*, by his own efforts, ascertain the philological meaning of any passage of Scripture; and when he has done that, he has done all that is needed to show what are the emphatic words of such passage.

The chief topics remaining to be considered are pause, modulation, and inflection. But they cannot be discussed by means of general precepts. Their disposition, in each several instance, depends on the character of the passage to be read; and their treatment, therefore, must be practical, and must be applied to the sentences or paragraphs selected for illustration.

I would like, now, briefly to call your attention to some remarks applicable generally to the manner and deportment of an officiating clergyman.

Of the difficulties that beset a young man at the commencement of his public duties in the Church, the first in order, and — while it continues — the first in importance, is *embarrassment*. Until he can divest himself of that, all his proficiency in elocution will be of little use; for, while under that incubus, he can not practise what he has learned of reading or speaking, any more than a man can walk or use his arms when he is bound hand and foot with cords. And, what makes the matter worse, he gets no sympathy from his audience; they make no allowance for his dilemma, — partly because they are not aware of it, and partly because they see no reason for it. The majority of a congregation will perceive the effect, but remain ignorant, or unmindful, of the cause; and the remainder, not being themselves embarrassed, cannot see why the clergyman should be so. But, for all that, he is so; it is in the nature of things that he should be so; and he is nearly helpless while he remains so. And another unfortunate feature of the case is, that embarrassment, above all other elocutionary obstacles, is the most difficult to control; because it depends on the nerves rather than on the will; and the nerves, in Shakespeare's phrase, "will not be commanded": they cannot even be reasoned with; and the only sure way of escaping their tyranny is, as an Irishman might say, to submit to it, as one does to sea-sickness, "until the tyranny be overpast." In other words, it is a kind of disease which the majority of clergymen must have once, though some will have it more lightly than others; and it can be treated only by palliatives. There is no prevention, and no summary cure. The best method of dealing with it is, perhaps, the novice's accustoming himself to the *sight* of a congregation, by sitting for a few Sundays in the chancel without officiating at all; and, after that, to undertake at first but a small portion of the service; and thus, by degrees, to familiarize himself to the situation, and to the sound of his own voice in the situation.

That suggestion, however, may be supererogatory on my part; for what I thus advise may already be an adopted custom. And, indeed, it is quite possible that many of my suggestions are not new, and might better have been spared. But, in submitting to you my views on elocution, it appeared to me the safer course to present the whole case, so far as I can; for if I were to assume that you are partly informed, and were I therefore to omit some things conjecturally, in deference to what you may already know, I might happen to omit so much as to leave you in doubt whether I myself understand what I have undertaken to communicate.

Assuming, now, that embarrassment has run its course, and is disposed of, — a result that necessarily depends on yourselves, for no one can materially aid you, — the next point is, a special study of the services of the day, so that you shall perfectly understand what you are to read, and how to read it. This study must be private; and, at whatever outlay of patient toil it may at first be undertaken, you should read, and re-read, aloud, every sentence, until you have disciplined yourselves, *compelled* yourselves, to bring your *reading* utterances into exact harmony with your *colloquial* tones. And, when you enter the church, you should entirely divest yourselves of that unfortunate, fatal, preconceived notion entertained by so many men, that your own natural voice is not suited to religious services.

Your next consideration is *audibleness;* to secure which you must not raise the key of the voice, but give more strength to it on its natural key;

and you may be assured, despite any previous impression to the contrary, that if your words are *distinctly articulated* on the true key, they will certainly make their way to the ears of the congregation. It would, however, be a wise precaution to secure the attendance of two or three friends in different parts of the church, whose special purpose shall be to ascertain whether you make yourselves heard; because, *some* additional strength of voice being necessary, no one can tell precisely how *much* is wanted, without more or less of practical experiment; and, besides, too much additional strength is as undesirable for the speaker, as too little is for the hearer. In this, as in other things, the happy medium is the desideratum. One thing, however, is to be noted: the additional strength should be *equally applied to every word*. Many clergymen whose delivery is what may be called of a proper *average* strength, distribute the strength so unequally as to fail of making themselves heard. The same thing occurs with many of us in conversation with a person partially deaf. We speak the larger and the more important words in a tone unnecessarily loud, and the monosyllables proportionately low, and our sentences become unintelligible for want of the small connecting words. Any familiar remark will illustrate this; for instance, " I am surprised at what you tell me." If that is spoken in the ordinary way, thus: [*repeated orally,*] each word is moderately pronounced, with a slight emphasis on the second syllable of " surprised."

But many persons, in saying that to one partially deaf, would vociferate "*prised*" and "*tell*," and so hurry and mumble every other syllable of the sentence that not one of them would be really audible to anybody; thus: [*repeated orally.*] The point to be secured is, a *sufficiency of strength with a uniformity of application.*

When a clergyman is reading the Lessons, he should remember that he *is* reading the Lessons, and keep his eyes fixed on the Bible. There are many readers who seem to practise on the problem, how much they can repeat while looking away from the book! and sometimes that really seems to be their chief object; the words they deliver, and the meaning and effect of the words, being subordinated to the solution of the problem. But no man can read well who divides his attention between the book and the people; and if he happens, as he often will, to "lose the place" while looking away from the book, he of course comes to a full stop, and breaks down altogether.

One more suggestion as to reading. *Never, never, never* allow the last word, or the several concluding words of a sentence, to be uttered in a whisper, or in any tone approaching a whisper. The universality of the habit of dropping one's voice on the last word or words of a sentence, is amazing. Even clergymen of long experience, and those who are aware of the frequency of the fault in themselves and in others, and who have temporarily cured themselves of it, will still perpetually relapse into it. Many men do this unconsciously; but the thing could hardly be so common if some clergymen did not persuade themselves that an occasional whisper is very impressive, and if each one who uses it did not flatter himself that *his* whisper is audible. I may remark, however, that, while a low tone at the end of a sentence is common to both readers and preachers, the actual whisper is usually reserved for the sermon. Nevertheless, as a rule, *no* whisper is audible in a church, and therefore no man can be justified in using it.

The delivery of a sermon is an exercise, in many respects, different from reading the Bible and Prayer Book; but, as an elocutionary exercise, it differs only by reason of its additional requirements. The meaning of the language is not, indeed, a necessary study; but that is only because a writer must be presumed to know his own meaning without study. A *knowledge* of meaning is indispensable in any case. Neither is it necessary or proper for a preacher to keep his eyes on his manuscript; on the contrary, he should dispense with his manuscript so far as he can without injury to a fluent utterance; for, other things being equal, every sentence of a sermon literally *spoken* has twice the power of the same words *read*. But, in every other particular, what has already been insisted on as essential to reading, is equally so to preaching.

Of requirements additional to those for reading,

it may be remarked, generally, that the most important of them appertain to the control, or want of control, of the voice; the reason for which is, that, in sermons, the various subjects to be considered, and the manner of their treatment, involve more development of personal interest and feeling than are ordinarily excited in reading the Bible or Prayer Book; and that the preacher, with all his efforts to make the printed service *practically* his own, seldom attains that object so completely as in dealing with what he has himself written, which is *really* his own. But — such is the perverseness of human nature — it often happens that just in proportion as a man's opportunities for doing well increase, his propensity to do ill, or to overdo, also increases; and hence, a clergyman, in the delivery of his own words, will go to extremes into which his discreet enthusiasm never betrays him when delivering the words of others. Thus, while, concurrently with other faults, the prevailing characteristic of reading is *monotony*, that of preaching is *extravagance*, — and the latter quality pertains chiefly to the management or control of the voice. It may be said, to be sure, that the whole art of elocution consists of the proper management and control of the voice; and, in the comprehensive sense of the words, that is true. But there are two kinds of such management and control: one is co-operative with the mind of the reader and the meaning of his language, which is the greater including the less; the other is a mere keeping of the voice in mechanical or physical subordination to the higher rules and principles of the art.

In this regard, then, let it be understood that a speaker should always retain full command of his voice. He must not allow his feelings to run away with it. Whether ministering to the afflicted, or entreating the careless; admonishing the impenitent, or denouncing the hardened transgressor, — whatever, indeed, may be the impulse, and however deeply he may be moved by it, he must still hold his voice under subjection. He must not permit it to be choked by sympathy, so that pathos becomes sobbing; nor overstrained by impetuosity, until energy is vulgarized into vociferation. There is no greater error in any relation of life, public or private, than an attempt to give force to language by intemperance, either of tone or gesticulation. Personal dignity disappears the moment that violence shows itself, and the influence of the speaker disappears with it; so that whenever he loses command of himself, he loses control of his audience. There is nothing in elocution so unexceptionally vicious, as violence of delivery: it is worse, even, than inaudibleness; for while the latter fatigues a congregation, the former disgusts them. Earnestness is commendable: even vehemence is sometimes endurable; but violence, *never*. The extreme exercise of a man's vocal power, which is the equivalent of roaring, or screaming, and which is — moderately speaking — *sometimes* practised in the pulpit; is a trespass on good taste, on every principle of elocution, and on the sanctity of the place, which nothing can excuse or palliate. A man who, in different capacities, is serving his Maker and his fellow-men, and who, in the name of the One, is exhorting the other, has *no right* to disregard the proprieties attaching to both relations. Neither is it wise to go still further and exaggerate even that extreme of indecorum into utter absurdity, as some men do, when their violence becomes undiscriminating: they seem to be, as it were, intoxicated with the reverberation of their own voices; they are agreeably astonished to find that they can make so much noise; and, by showering their stentorian utterances at random, they give fearful prominence to an *and* or a *but*, as often as to a more important word. And another thing may be mentioned. When the declamatory afflatus is at its zenith, the speaker, finding that his utmost vocal efforts fall short of his enthusiasm, reinforces the power of voice with the power of gesticulation; and he brings that part of his performance to a climax with a violent slap of his hand, or blow of his fist, on his sermon, or on the Bible or the cushion that holds it. He thus, in Hamlet's phrase, " suits the action to the word," because both are tempestuous: but he raises more *dust* than sympathy.

Now, if clergymen did but know it, or would but know it, every time they indulge in this extravagance, they not only defeat their immediate object; but they injure their position with their audience by betraying a weakness, which they would do much better to conceal.

In conclusion of the requisites to the proper delivery of a sermon, I would say a few words on *gesticulation*, — as to which, the safest course for a novice is to *avoid it altogether;* at least as a matter of either experiment or study. Remember, as a controlling fact, that there is no *need* of gestures at all. No elocutionary rule *requires* them, and if there is any rule *about* them, it is a rule whose sole office is *prohibition*. It enjoins simply this, — that *inappropriate* gesture shall be avoided: and one reason for its going no further is to be found in the nature of the case: for no precept could be so framed as to include all the varieties of proper action in the pulpit, and to provide for the still greater variety of circumstances that would affect its application. Besides, what is improper cannot easily be known to the preacher himself, because he cannot see himself: the congregation are the sole witnesses and judges of that. But if a clergyman will *never study*, or *premeditate*, or *privately practise* a gesture; and, as an invariable rule, will permit his hands and arms to obey nothing but his internal impulse at the moment, independently of how the thing may *look*, he will never go far wrong.

A very disagreeable habit, and by no means an uncommon one of either young or old clergymen, is a frequently repeated motion of the right arm, always describing the same circle, or semicircle, or angular or curved line, uniform in extent of feet and inches, and made without the slightest reference to the words it accompanies. The action is usually ungraceful, because it is studied; and it has the effect on a spectator that anything obviously artificial will always have. There are many other gestures with one arm, or both, equally stereotyped and equally vicious; but every gesture that is premeditated, or uniform, should be strenuously avoided.

And — to bring this matter of pulpit deportment to an end — I will add that some clergymen have a habit of looking in only one direction while delivering their sermons. The object of their attention — excepting, of course, the manuscript — is the ceiling, or the floor, or the organ, or a column on the right or left; or, a part of the congregation on one side, or the other, or in front; but in each particular instance, the one object is the only object looked at. This is a habit that seems to indicate either apathy or embarrassment on the part of a preacher. The only proper course for a clergyman in the pulpit, after giving the necessary attention to his manuscript, is to direct his eyes easily and occasionally to every part of the congregation, so that every person present may have reason to consider himself individually addressed.

I would like now to make two suggestions about sermons themselves, which are not in any way connected with their delivery.

The first is not very important, and it is merely a matter of taste. A great number, perhaps a majority, of clergymen state where the text is to be found, then read it, and then *repeat* the announcement in both particulars. The only effect of this, so far as I can judge, is to encourage an old and very bad, but now comparatively infrequent custom on the part of the congregation, of *verifying* the preacher's announcement by looking up the text in their Bibles, gravely reading it, and handing the book up or down the pew that others may also verify the announcement. If the preacher would *wait* while all this is in progress, there would be less impropriety, though no less superfluity, in the custom; but the preacher does *not* wait, and therefore the only effect of the custom is a general interruption. But the *repetition* by the preacher is itself superfluous. It is a sort of assumption of the importance of a text *as* appertaining to a sermon; whereas, the importance of a text is intrinsic, independently of the sermon. A preacher may, and may not, make an important *use* of a text in the course of his sermon, but he can *give* it no importance by announcing it.

My second suggestion relates to the *theme* of a sermon. It is a matter of common observation that young clergymen almost always overshoot the mark in their initiatory efforts at writing for the pulpit. They are apt to attempt *too much*. Instead of contenting themselves with expounding the plain precepts of the Gospel, which alone they are called on to consider, and which they are perfectly able to discuss, they are prone to undertake some new phase of a doctrinal point; or, to expatiate on some of the mysteries of the Gospel dispensation; or, to attempt fine writing, and to sprinkle their paragraphs with large words and figures of rhetoric; or, to aim at originality, or at some other thing not easily attained and not worth attaining. They do, in short, just what young men do because they *are* young men, what a majority of their predecessors *have* done, and what they will themselves *cease* to do, whenever they cease to be young men. And the object of this suggestion is, to point out a common fault that can readily be discerned and identified, and which would therefore be much better avoided at first, than be left to the chances of being cured, or *not* cured, by experience.

I have now offered to your consideration all that my limited time permits of elocutionary principles, independently of practical illustrations; and it all comes to but this at last, — that a student of elocution must be substantially his own teacher.

INDEX.

	Page
A hearty meal	65
Abbess	22
Abuse	164
Actor	22
Actress	22
Addison	5, 53
Affectation	43, 183
Alford, Dean,	8, 75, 89, 93, 102, 112
Alternative	45
Alison	72
Ambassador	22
Americanism	89
Amour	159
Analysis of a sentence	184
Anywheres	25
Apprehend	86
Archæology	105
Astrology	105
At length	50
Attorney, Attornies	91
Audibleness	199
Au fait	103
Author, Authoress	21
Baroness	22
Beckman, James W.	137
Benefactor, Benefactress	22
Beside, Besides	28
Blackwood's Magazine	24
Blair	5
Book Genesis, The	57
Bourn	96
Brace	33
Build	161
Bulwer	63
Burke	54
Business	110
But that	59
Byron	72, 79
Case, Casket, Coffin	85
Casuality	19
Centre	161

	Page
Chancellor	158
Chesterfield	54
Cibber	90
Craniology	105
Coleridge	19
Collate	21
Colton	184
Comparative adjectives	69
Contrasting adjectives	69
Conchology	105
Conductress	23
Consequence	36
Controversialist	12
Conversationalist, etc.	17
Correspond	62
Counsellor	158
Countess	22
Couple	32, 150
Curious	51, 158
David Copperfield	96
Dean's English, The	135
Debase	24, 34
Debasement	35
Deceiving	104
Defence, Defense	148
Delivery of a Sermon	217
Demean	24, 34
Demeanour	34
Democratic Review, The	139
Deride	34
Deportment of a clergyman	212
De trop	103
Device, Devise	164
Dickens	24, 46, 95
Directly	107
Directress	23
Discriminate	50
Distil	158
Distinguish	50
Doddridge	86
Donate	20
Donkey, Donkies	94

226 INDEX.

Drive 84
Dropping the voice . . 216
Dryden 5
Dulness 157

Earnestness 219
Easy 110
Economist 15
Edinburgh Review . . 16, 117
Either 40
Embarrassment . . . 212
Emphasis 199
Emphasis overdone . . 211
Empress 22
Enamour 159
Enrol 156
Enthral 156
Epithet 48
Error 184
Everett 21, 55
Exceptionable . . . 87
Excuse 164
Exhibit 68
Experimentalize . . . 17

Famous 160
Favour 159
Few, a 89
Figure 102
First, the 108
Firstly 24
From hence, thence, whence 99
From out 99
Fulfil 157
Fulness 157
Furious 160

Garrick 192, 193
General Grant . . 21, 63
Genesis, The Book . . 57
Geology 105
Gesticulation . . . 221
Gibbon 5, 79
Goldsmith 64
Governor 22
Good writers . . 141, 143
Graduated 102
Guide, Guard, Guilt . . 161

Hamlet 92
Hardy 110
Holmes, Oliver Wendell . 140
Honour 159
Hostilize 86
Humble 111
Hunter 22

I never mean to . . . 96
Ignorance 184
Imitation 188
Importance 86
In our midst . . . 65
In so far 61
In that 60
Infinitive Mood . . . 72
Inspectress 23
Instal 156
Instil 158
Invite 68
Irving, Washington . 54, 156
Issue 84

Jenkins and Jones . . 78
Jeffrey 72, 90
Jeopardize 11
John Halifax . . . 17
Johnson 6, 20, 85, 36, 53, 72, 143
Journal 82
Junius 5
Justified 75

Kean, Edmund . . . 185

Lady 30, 32
Latham 5
Lazy 110
Leniency 15
Lexicographer, A . . 143
London Times, The . 77, 120
London Athenæum . . 51
London Morning Chronicle . 120
Logy, the termination . 105
Looked beautifully . . 49
Lustre 161
Lyttleton 54

Macaulay . . . 5, 12, 120
Macready . . . 185, 194
Macbeth 87, 92
Maintain 75
Make no more noise than you
  can help 88
Manageress 23
Many a 89
Marchioness 22
Marsh, George P. 18, 70, 71, 80
Materialistic . . . 18
Matinée 103
Mechanical style . . 193
Meteorology . . . 105
Milton 25, 53
Mineralogy . . . 105
Misapprehend . . . 68

Misconceive	68
Misjudge	68
Misunderstand	68
Mistaken	66
Money, Monies	93
Monkey, Monkies	94
Moon, G. Washington	80, 135
Most	52
Mould, Moult	164
Mutual	111
Mutual friend	46
Nation, The	18, 70, 80
Neither	40
Never	88
Newspapers	8, 55
New York Evening Post	21, 28, 139
Ninth Commandment	204
Nowheres	25
Of all others	64
Offence, Offense	148
Officeress	23
One	58
One half	87
Only	100
Opened up	98
Orate	21
Ornithology	105
Osteology	195
Our mutual friend	46
Ovate	21
Over his signature	47
Overtake	68
Pair	33
Paley	14
Paragraph Bible	195
Paraphernalia	44
Patron, Patroness	22
Pause, for emphasis	205
Peculiar	52
Pen	63
Permit	68
Perpetual	111
Philology	105
Phrenology	105
Physiology	105
Pincate	86
Plead	102
Plough	160
Poet, Poetess	22
Possessive Case, The	74
Practice, Practise	163
Predicate	38
Predict	86

Prescott	54
Pretence, Pretense	148
Preventative	19
Priest, Priestess	22
Princess	22
Profit	150
Proffer	150
Progress	89
Promise	107
Prophet	22
Prophecy, Prophesy	164
Reading the Lessons	216
Rebel	92
Recommend	68
Reformer, A	143
Repetition of texts	223
Reverend, The	56
Resurrected	86
Richelieu	63
Ride	84
Rising inflection	206, 209
Rotatory	19
Round Table, The	80, 167
School Readers	174
Scott, Walter	147
Secretaryess	23
Sentences	103
Sepulchre	161
Separatist	15
Serious	160
Should have regretted his having been	73
Singeress	23
Smart	19
Smollett	54
Somewheres	25
Southey	59, 72
South, Dr.	25
Span	33
Stand-point	25
Start-point	26
Stopping	65
Superintendentess	23
Supple	150
Sweat of his brow	98
Talkeress	23
That	60
Theatre	161
Theme of a Sermon	223
Theology	195
To the muzzle	85
Tony Butler	65
Toward	24

Treasureress 23	Was, for *is*, etc. . . . 101
Trench 41, 59, 60, 61, 72, 74, 109	Weary 110
Trollope, Anthony . . 65	Webster, Daniel . . 55
Try and 104	Webster, Noah 14, 20, 30, 89, 66, 95
	Webster's Dictionary . 14, 71
Underhanded . . . 19	Wharf, wharfs, wharves . 106
Underminded . . . 20	Whispers 217
Universe 83	White, Richard Grant . 21
Usage of good writers . . 3	Whose 79
Usual 111	Widow lady . . . 58
Variety of tones . . . 195	Widow woman . . . 58
Vehemence . . . 219	Wife 30
Verses, the Bible in . . 196	Wilson 72
View-point . . . 27	Without 63
Violence 219	Woman 31
Voice injured by monotony 199	Worcester 16, 48
	Worcester's Dictionary . 166
Waitress 23	Writeress 28
Walker 154	
Walkeress 23	Yoke 83
Walpole 54	You are mistaken . . 66

THE END.

Widdleton's Editions of Choice Standard Works

REVISED EDITION

OF

Trench on the Study of Words.

LECTURES ADDRESSED (ORIGINALLY) TO THE PUPILS OF THE DIOCESAN TRAINING-SCHOOL, WINCHESTER. By RICHARD CHENEVIX TRENCH, D. D. The Thirtieth American from the last English Edition, enlarged and revised by the Author. 12mo, cloth, 248 pp., $1.25.

"Language is the armory of the human mind, and at once contains the trophies of its past, and the weapons of its future conquests."

"This is one of the most instructive, as well as interesting books, and we particularly recommend it to those who are under the impression that the study of mere words must necessarily be uninteresting. Professor Trench has made what has heretofore been considered a dry and repulsive study interesting to all intelligent persons, even though they may be ignorant of any but the English tongue."

For sale at the principal Bookstores throughout the country and mailed by Publisher on receipt of price.

W. J. WIDDLETON, PUBLISHER,

New York.

THE
STUDENT'S MYTHOLOGY;

A COMPENDIUM OF

Greek, Roman, Egyptian, Assyrian, Persian, Hindoo, Chinese, Thibetan, Scandinavian, Celtic, Aztec, and Peruvian Mythologies, in accordance with Standard Authorities.

Arranged for the use of Schools and Academies by C. A. WHITE.

(PREPARED BY REQUEST FOR THE SCHOOLS OF THE S. H., AND REVISED AT GEORGETOWN COLLEGE.)

A handsome 12mo volume, 315 *pp., cloth,* $1.25.

———

THE STUDENT'S MYTHOLOGY is a practical work, prepared by an experienced teacher, and submitted to the decisive test of the School-room, having been in use in "manuscript" for three years, and meeting with great favor from teachers and pupils, — preferring it, even in that inconvenient form, to other text-books on the subject.

Copies were eagerly sought by other institutions, and the Compiler consented to its publication.

GEORGETOWN COLLEGE, GEORGETOWN, D. C.

"THE STUDENT'S MYTHOLOGY is a work every way fitting to be placed in the hands of the class for whom it was prepared, and indeed will be read with pleasure by any one. In its pages nothing will be found of a nature to offend delicacy; while its limpid style, and its numerous poetical and historical illustrations, cannot but attract the student, improve the taste, and inform the mind. It is learned without being heavy, and comprehensive without being lengthy."

JNO. S. SUMNER, S. J.

———

For sale at principal Bookstores throughout the country, and mailed by Publisher on receipt of price.

W. J. WIDDLETON, PUBLISHER,
New York.

Widdleton's Editions of Choice Standard Works

Disraeli's Complete Works

THE AUTHORIZED AND COMPLETE EDITION,

Edited, with Notes, by his Son, the Right Hon. B. DISRAELI Ex-Premier of England. In 9 vols. crown 8vo. Large clear type, on fine toned paper, bound in handsome library style in extra cloth, comprising:—

THE CURIOSITIES OF LITERATURE. 4 vols. . $7.00

THE AMENITIES OF LITERATURE. 2 vols. . 3 50

THE CALAMITIES AND QUARRELS OF AUTHORS. 2 vols. 3 50

THE LITERARY CHARACTER. 1 vol. . . . 2.25

Any of the works sold separately as above, or the entire set of nine volumes in a case for $15.00; half calf, $30.00.

This set of books contains what may be called the cream of reading and research, from the time of Dr. Johnson to our own, and of the superiority of this edition there is no room for question; a comparison with the English,— crowded into six volumes of small type,— decides at a glance.

For sale at the principal Bookstores throughout the country, and sent by mail or express, on receipt of price by

W. J. WIDDLETON, PUBLISHER,

27 Howard Street, New York

Widdleton's Editions of Choice Standard Works

Charles Lamb's Works.

The complete works of "The Gentle Elia," corrected and revised, with a sketch of his life, by THOMAS NOON TALFORD, and a fine steel portrait.

This is the most complete, and a very elegant edition of LAMB. Printed in large clear type, on choice tinted paper. 5 vols. crown 8vo., cloth, cut or uncut edges, $9.00; half calf or half Turkey morocco, $18. Each set of books in a box.

LAMB'S ESSAYS OF ELIA. A new edition, on tinted paper. In 1 vol. crown 8vo, cloth, cut or uncut edges, $1.75; half calf, or half Turkey morocco, $3.50.

LAMB'S ELIANA. Containing the hitherto uncollected Writings of CHARLES LAMB. In 1 vol. crown 8vo, cloth, cut or uncut edges, $1.75; half calf or half Turkey morocco, $3.50.

"This gentle Lamb — Heaven be praised for ordaining him the fittest, as it is the sweetest, of names! — was one whose daily life grew more beautiful as one came nearer to it and measured it more carefully.

"The world will be much older than it is yet, before an intelligent man or woman can be pardoned for asking, "Who was Charles Lamb?" And yet, because we know him so well, we are the more willing to know him better; we cannot learn so much as to be content not to know more. There is no healthier sign of a sound literary taste than this tender attachment for such a writer as Lamb. These dainty, exquisite pages — of which nothing too good can be said, and for which book-lovers cannot too heartily thank the conscientious publisher — breathe a sweetness, a fragrance, as fine as the breezes of May, and as good for the appetent soul." — *Chicago Evening Journal.*

For sale at principal Bookstores throughout the country, and mailed by Publisher on receipt of price.

W. J. WIDDLETON, PUBLISHER,
New York.

www.ingramcontent.com/pod-product-compliance
Lightning Source LLC
Chambersburg PA
CBHW031745230426
43669CB00007B/496